FOLK METAPHYSICS

Mystical Meanings in Traditional
Folk Songs and Spirituals

FOLK
METAPHYSICS

Mystical Meanings
in Traditional Folk Songs
and Spirituals

CHARLES UPTON

SOPHIA PERENNIS

SAN RAFAEL, CA

First published in the USA
by Sophia Perennis
© Charles Upton 2008

Series editor: James R. Wetmore

For information, address:
Sophia Perennis, P.O. Box 151011
San Rafael, CA 94915
sophiaperennis.com

Library of Congress Cataloging-in-Publication Data

Upton, Charles, 1948–
Folk metaphysics: mystical meanings in traditional
folk songs and spirituals / Charles Upton.

p. cm.
ISBN 978-1-59731-077-2 (pbk: alk. paper)
1. Folk songs—Religious aspects. I. Title
ML3921.8.F65U67   2008
782.42162'130112—dc22   2008003157

ACKNOWLEDGMENTS

For *The Lady Gay* and the verse from *Am I Born to Die?*, Mason Brown and Chipper Thompson said: '"traditional" means "free"'.

For the lines from his *Bow Down*, John Herrmann said: "OK by me."

The City Lights people gave kind permission for me to reprint Lew Welch's *The Song Mt. Tamalpais Sings*, for free.

I paid a little fee to Gary Snyder for the right to reprint the poem from his *Cold Mountain Poems*, and the lines from his poem *Regarding Wave*.

I paid another tiny fee to G. Schirmer, Inc. & Associated Music Publishers, Inc., and they told me to say:

Piri-Miri-Dictum-Domini
By John Jacob Niles
Copyright ©1936 (Renewed) by G. Schirmer, Inc. (ASCAP)
International Copyright Secured. All Rights Reserved.
Reprinted by Permission

I tried my best to find out who might hold the copyright to *Poet in New York* by Federico García Lorca, translated by Ben Bellitt, for the passages quoted from *The Duende: Theory and Divertissement*, but no luck. Let the copyright holder contact me, or Sophia Perennis, if he or she ever sees this book.

The passages from *A Beginner's Guide to Constructing the Universe: Mathematical Archetypes of Nature, Art, and Science*, by Michael S. Schneider, are reprinted by permission of Harper-Collins Publishers.

Jean Ritchie and Geordie Music kindly granted me their "house-keeping terms" for reprinting her two songs; the credit lines appear with the lyrics in the body of the book.

Permission to reprint the lines from the poem *Elijah Browning* from Edgar Lee Masters' *Spoon River Anthology* were graciously granted by his son Hilary Masters, who told me to say:

> Elijah Browning from Spoon River Anthology by Edgar Lee Masters, originally published by the Macmillan Company. Permission by Hilary Masters.

Permission to quote passages from the writings of Ananda Kentish Coomaraswamy was kindly granted by Peter Coomaraswamy, his grandson.

CONTENTS

INTRODUCTION

IN THIS BOOK I do my best to throw light on the spiritual meanings and the metaphysical world-view hidden in certain traditional Appalachian, English, Scottish and Cornish folk songs, as well as in a few Negro spirituals. Not all traditional folk songs contain such meanings; a song like "Mattie Groves" is pretty much about what it appears to be about—seduction, adultery and revenge. And only a few spirituals have a *hidden* spiritual meaning beneath the more obvious one. But certain songs—virtually any song that has a riddle in it, for example—are deliberately constructed to transmit a great mass of spiritual lore in a dense, compacted form. I don't claim that my interpretations are the only valid ones; the meaning of every true symbol, every true myth, is inexhaustible. In some cases I've used a particular song as a kind of key or catalyst to tap the spiritual lore-hoard of the human race. But it is crystal clear to me that many traditional songs are packed with explicit spiritual doctrine, and that the people who wrote them knew exactly what they were talking about.

The language that the lyrics I will explicate below is written in, is *mythopoeia,* which I define as "the expression of metaphysical doctrines in symbolic rather than discursive language." Greek philosophy is discursive; the *Iliad* and the *Odyssey*—as well as *Ezekiel* and *The Book of Job*—are mythopoetic. Mythopoeia, such as we often find in myths, fairy tales, riddles and folk songs, is designed to project virtual but quite specific metaphysical knowledge into those areas of the mind—the emotional, intuitive, "right brain" areas—that don't depend on logical discourse. But when the rational, discursive part of the mind is also open to metaphysical intuition, rather than simply operating on its own premises, it can produce the kind of exegesis that throws a fully conscious light on the metaphysics hidden in mythopoetic compositions. That's what I hope I've done in this book. The reverse is also possible: As metaphysical discourse can be an *hermeneutic* of mythopoeia (Plato, in his dialogues, provides this kind of hermeneutic for a number of Greek myths), so mythopoeia can *epitomize* metaphysics. And that's what I believe some of the unsung singers of traditional folk lyrics have done: they've compressed a large body of *conscious* metaphysics and spiritual lore into tight little musical narratives or sets of mystical riddles.

But who, exactly, placed those meanings there? Christians? Pagans? Somebody else? This is a hard question to ask, and one I am not fully qualified to answer (if anyone is). My job, as I see it, is to dig up the artifacts and describe their structure; I leave it up to those better trained as cultural historians than I am to do the radio-carbon dating and speculate on who buried them in the first place. My approach is more like that of an astronomer than a historian. An astronomer observing the constellation of Scorpio will see that the star Antares has a reddish tinge to it. But if later he reads that some medieval Muslim astronomer also noticed the redness of Antares, and remarked on it, will he be led to believe that the redness of the star he sees through his telescope is the product of medieval Muslim ideas? Obviously not. He knows the true color of the star because he is observing the actual star itself, and therefore concludes that the Muslim astronomer must have been looking at the same star. My basic treatment of spiritual lore, or what I recognize as such, is quite similar: God is real, the metaphysical order is real, the spiritual life is real; consequently the spiritual lore of different religions, different cultures, different historical periods will show inevitable similarities because they are all contemplating the same changeless Reality. The crystal structure of the diamond was octahedral in 4000 BC, and is still octahedral today; so observations of the structure of diamonds made 6000 years ago are not necessarily irrelevant. And when it comes to spiritual realities, certain ancient observations might be even more accurate than modern ones, since the conceptual and perceptual sets of the ancients, their "microscopes" and "telescopes," were designed specifically to investigate spiritual realities, as ours are more often designed to investigate material ones. And because I take the metaphysical order and the spiritual life as real, as well as seeing in them the specific context that allows the meanings I believe I've found in traditional songs to reveal themselves, I must begin by saying something about what is called the Primordial Tradition, the universal metaphysics of the human race, as well as about the Spiritual Path, the way the truth of metaphysics and the reality of God have been realized and actualized in all traditional cultures. In this I follow the scriptures and the enlightened saints and sages of all the "high" religions, particularly (through not exclusively) as re-presented by the writers of what is called the Traditionalist or Perennialist school: René Guénon, Ananda Coomaraswamy, Frithjof Schuon, Titus Burckhardt, Martin Lings, Marco Pallis, Prof. Huston Smith, Prof. Seyyed Hossein Nasr, Rama Coomaraswamy, Whitall Perry, Mark Perry, Prof. William Chittick, Prof. Vincent Cornell, Prof. James Cutsinger, Lord Northbourne, Charles LeGai Eaton, Prof. Joseph Epes Brown, Elemire Zolla, William Stoddart, and many others.

Ananda K. Coomaraswamy, the great Anglo-Indian writer on metaphysics and traditional art (a native of Sri Lanka who ended up as curator in the department of Asiatic Art of the Boston Museum of Fine Arts), has this to say about the metaphysical dimension of folklore:

> [By] "folklore" we mean that whole and consistent body of culture which has been handed down, not in books but by word of mouth and in practice, from time beyond the reach of historical research, in the form of legends, fairy tales, ballads, games, toys, crafts, medicine, agriculture, and other rites, and forms of organization, especially those we call tribal. This is a cultural complex independent of national and even racial boundaries, and of remarkable similarity throughout the world. . . . The content of folklore is metaphysical. Our failure to recognize this is primarily due to our own abysmal ignorance of metaphysics and of its technical terms. . . . Folklore ideas are the form in which metaphysical doctrines are received by the people and transmitted by them. In its popular form, a given doctrine may not always have been understood, but so long as the formula is faithfully transmitted it remains understandable; "superstitions," for the most part, are no mere delusions, but formulae of which the meaning has been forgotten. . . . We are dealing with the relics of an ancient

wisdom, as valid now as it ever was. . . . We shall only be able to understand the astounding uniformity of the folklore motifs all over the world, and the devoted care that has everywhere been taken to ensure their correct transmission, if we approach these mysteries (for they are nothing less) in the spirit in which they have been transmitted ("from the Stone Age until now")—with the confidence of little children, indeed, but not the childish self-confidence of those who hold that wisdom was born with themselves. The true folklorist must be not so much a psychologist as a theologian and metaphysician, if he is to "understand his material". . . . Nor can anything be called a science of folklore, but only a collection of data, that considers only the formulae and not their doctrine. . . .[1]

Since the subject of this book is folk ballads in their particular relationship to the spiritual Path, it is my duty to provide the necessary context Coomaraswamy calls for—in terms of cultural history, certainly, but also in terms of theological dogma and metaphysical doctrine. As for cultural history, I have attempted (further on in this Introduction, and elsewhere) to situate the songs I've investigated within their greater aesthetic and cultural context—Irish, British, and especially American, which itself is set within the greater context of the inescapable bond between the world of the living and that of the ancestors, the tribes and nations of the human dead. I've shown how these songs relate to the work of other American singers and songwriters, both traditional and popular, as well as to American poets such as Walt Whitman, Emily Dickinson, Edgar Allen Poe, Edgar Lee Masters, Gary Snyder and Lew Welch. But I've also situated that cultural context itself within the greater theological and metaphysical frame-of-reference from which I habitually write, which has led me to some interesting encounters with questions like: "How does nostalgia relate to the spiritual Path; is it a help or a hindrance?" If we view a culture only in its own "historical," "sociological" or "cultural" terms, we contract into pedantry (hopefully

---

1. *Coomaraswamy, Selected Papers: Traditional Art and Symbolism*; Bollingen Series LXXXIX, ed. Roger Lipsey (Princeton: Princeton Univ. Press, 1977), pp 286; 287; 306; 369–370; 536.

turning up some useful and factual information on the way down). But if we see it as one expression of the Eternal Human Form as God created it, then it begins to expand and give off light, like a star being born; it reveals its essence.

THE WAY THINGS ARE

The following is a summary of the fundamental world-view, the set of *root assumptions,* that I work from. It is that "the way things are," on the deepest level, has always been known. We are used to thinking that human knowledge doubles every year, that "further research" will always expand the boundaries of what is known by the human race. But knowledge of the way things are cannot be expanded. Research can add nothing to it. It is all there, full and compact, in the first moment it is seen, which was the first moment the first human being opened his eyes—both his two outer eyes, and the single Eye of his Heart. Such knowledge can be learned, it can be translated, re-translated and commented upon, but it can't be *added to.* It is not the kind of knowledge we *possess,* but the kind of knowledge we are *made of.* The human form is deliberately and specifically designed to know this knowledge—and what it knows, it also is.

In earlier times—some of them truly prehistoric—everything in our man-made environment was designed to remind us of, and teach us about, the way things are. And we (most of us, that is) could still look at the natural world and read it like a book; we could do this because we knew Who wrote that book, and could feel His presence everywhere. Not everybody always knew the way things are, but *somebody* always did. And somebody always will; the day the last one of us passes away who knows the way things are will be the end of this world.

This ancient and universal knowledge is called the Primordial Tradition. This tradition is unanimous in its doctrines, and speaks a single language. A time came, however, when this language began to be forgotten. The story of this is told in the Bible as the fall of the Tower of Babel. Before the tower fell, everybody spoke the same language, but afterwards, they could no longer understand each other. The different "languages" they started to speak at that time were actually different religions (and, later, different philosophies). Every true religion has the whole story of the way things are stuck away somewhere in its scriptures and traditions, but since knowledge of the original language of the human race had now been lost, fewer and fewer people could read the whole story in its later, translated versions.

But now that we are getting near to the end of the world, that original language is starting to come back. We can't really live like our ancestors did in the Garden of Eden or the Golden Age, seeing God everywhere and basing all our cultural and social forms on this universal vision; but we can begin to better understand the various later translations of the universal story. The Primordial Tradition alone can't save us, it can't be a spiritual Path for us; only the true and revealed religions of the world can do that. The nourishing fruit of the Tree of Religion grows on the branches, not on the trunk. But the Primordial Tradition, the original story of the way things are, told in its original language, can let us see (God willing) deep, deep into those religions, all the way back to the Garden before the Fall.

Spiritual truth is told in three basic languages. The first is the language of philosophy and metaphysics; the classical Greeks were pretty good at that one. The second is the language of myth and symbol, the language called *mythopoeia* above, sometimes spoken in words, sometimes written, sometimes expressed in music, songs, dances, statues, paintings, buildings, weapons, clothes, utensils, tools, dreams… All the peoples of the world spoke this language at one time, and some still do; the Jews were masters of the verbal form of it. And the third language is the language of *presence*: a strong and wise and good human being—a saint, in other words— shines with that strength and wisdom and goodness, sometimes in words, but most of all in silence. As one Hasidic Jew said of the holy Maggid of Mezritch, "I did not go to the Maggid to learn Torah from his mouth, but to watch him tie his bootlaces."

So the Primordial Tradition mostly comes down to us through the religions of the world. But there are still remnants of this universal wisdom that come to us through other channels, some of them almost inconceivably ancient. In myth, folklore, folk songs, riddles, superstitions, hand gestures, jokes and dances, the way we nod "yes" and shake our heads "no," great secrets are sometimes hidden—and that is certainly true of some British, Scottish and Appalachian folk songs: certainly not all of them, but definitely some of them. The very language of such songs (like the language of daily life in older times, and even in our own time if we knew half of what we are really saying) is filled with and constructed according to metaphysical concepts. Take, for example, the song "Wildwood Flower":

> I will twine with my mingles
>   Of raven black hair
> With the roses so red
>   And the lilies so fair
>
> . . . .
>
> I will dance I will sing
>   And my life shall be gay
> I will charm every heart
>   In its crown I will sway
> I woke from my dreamin'
>   All idols was clay
> And all portions of lovin'
>   Had all flown away
>
> . . . .
>
> He taught me to love him
>   And called me his flower
> That was bloomin' to cheer him
>   Through life's weary hour
> How I long to see him
>   And regret the dark hour
> He's gone and neglected
>   His frail wildwood flower

Without some understanding of this older, more metaphysical way of looking at things, the lines "I will charm every heart / In its crown I will sway" sound half like nonsense. We see a little girl, with her raven black hair, swaying like a hoola dancer inside some kind of cardboard crown covered with gold paper, as if in a scene from a grammar school play. But "sway" actually means *rule* (as in "the King held sway"). So first we have a *heart*; then a *crown* within or upon that heart; and finally a figure ruling or holding *sway* within it. This is taken directly from a spiritual anthropology that was once universally understood, on some level or other, by every traditional culture. The *heart* is the center of the soul or psyche; the *crown* is what the Muslim Sufis and the Eastern Orthodox Christian Hesychasts call "the Eye of the Heart," corresponding to the Greek term *Nous*—the Uncreated Intellect that knows God directly just as the eye knows light. And the only One with both the right and the power to hold sway within the crown of the heart is God himself— not some teasing little coquette who twines *roses* (eros) and *lilies* (virginity) in her *mingles* (locks) of raven black hair. (On the highest level, the roses are God's immanence within His creation, and the lilies His total transcendence of it.) One of the Greek Sirens was named *Thelxinoê*, meaning "Charming to the Mind"-- the *Nous*. According to the bardic conventions of Persian Sufi poetry, the dark, entangling locks of the Beloved (God) are His outer expressions or manifestations in which we become entangled, "hung up" or *locked*; they are His "lover's wiles" that both prevent us from escaping Him and involve us in relatively peripheral issues and fascinations, when (erotically speaking) we should be seeking the ultimate goal. It is because the little girl in the song wants to charm every heart to the point of replacing the image of God in them that she gets into trouble; it is this sacrilegious presumptuousness that leads to her abandonment by her lover, and the dark hour of her regret.

The French metaphysical writer René Guénon, who died in 1951, had this to say about the metaphysical aspects of folklore, in his book *Symbols of the Sacred Science*:

> The very conception of 'folklore' as it is commonly understood rests on the radically false idea that there exist 'popular creations', spontaneous products of the masses; and one can immediately see the close relationship between this way of looking at things and 'democratic' prejudices. As has been quite rightly said [by Luc Benoist], 'the profound interest of all so-called popular traditions lies above all in the fact that they are not popular in

origin'; and we would add that if, as is almost always the case, we are dealing with elements that are traditional in the true sense of the word, however deformed, diminished or fragmentary they may sometimes be, and with things of real symbolic value, then their origin, far from being popular, is not even human. What may be popular is uniquely the fact of 'survival' when these elements come from traditional forms that have disappeared. . . . The people thus preserve, without understanding them, the debris of ancient traditions sometimes even reaching back to a past too remote to be determined and which is therefore consigned to the obscure domain of 'prehistory'; and in so doing they function as a more or less 'subconscious' collective memory, the content of which has manifestly come from somewhere else. What may seem most astonishing is that, when we go to the root of the matter, the things so conserved are found to contain in more or less veiled form a considerable body of esoteric data, that is, what is least 'popular' in essence, and this fact of itself suggests an explanation that we will lay out in a few words. *When a traditional form is on the verge of extinction, its last representatives may very well deliberately entrust to this collective memory of which we have just spoken what would otherwise be irrevocably lost. This, in short, is the only way to save what can, at least in some measure, be saved; and, at the same time, the natural incomprehension of the masses is a sufficient guarantee that whatever possesses an esoteric character will not be despoiled in the process but will remain as a sort of witness to the past for those in later times who may be capable of understanding it* [italics mine].[2]

Guénon does sound a bit elitist here; the traditional folk may not know what the great sage knows, but they do know something of real value, which is how to live a traditional life. (The "folk," remember, are not the same as the "masses" now largely controlled and manipulated by the mass media.) But though the folk may hold a particular idea hidden within them, only the artist (either folk-artist or *artiste* of the intelligentsia) can cast it into a form that can be clearly understood (by some) or simply passed on without

---

2. *Symbols of Sacred Science* (Hillsdale, NY: Sophia Perennis, 2004), pp 24–25.

corruption (by others). Nowadays, though, it seems like we either have to understand everything or lose everything; now that the unconscious folk memory has largely been replaced by the internet, everything—it seems—either has to get more and more painfully explicit, or else descend into idiocy and forgetfulness.

THE SPIRITUAL PATH

Doctrine relating directly to The Way Things Are has to do first with the science of *ontology*, the study of Being, and secondarily with the science of *cosmology*, the study of the universe not as a set of physical objects and processes but as a creation or manifestation of God. In terms of the spiritual Path, these sciences exist to inform and support a third science, that of *anthropology*—not the kind of anthropology we study in college, however, which is all about the practices and beliefs of various cultures, often primitive ones (cultural anthropology), or about the biological "evolution" of early man or the differences between the races (physical anthropology). *Spiritual* anthropology has to do not with what human beings have believed, or the surface variations in the human form, but with what a human being really *is*. The first axiom of spiritual anthropology is: "A human being is created in the image and likeness of God." The second axiom is: "The intrinsic duty of a human being, therefore, is to *be* the presence of God on earth, to function as the channel that unites the visible universe with its invisible Source." In the words of Genesis 1:26; 28:

> And God said: Let us make man in our image, and after our likeness: and let them have dominion over the fish of the sea and over the fowl of the air, and over the cattle, and over all the earth, and over every creeping thing that creepeth on the earth. . . . and God said unto them: Be fruitful, and multiply, and replenish the earth, and subdue it.

And in the words of the Qur'an (33:72):

> We offered the Trust unto the heavens and the earth and the hills, but they shrank from bearing it and were afraid of it. And man assumed it. Lo! He hath proved a tyrant and a fool.

According to Eastern Orthodox theologians, there is a difference between being in the *image* of God, and being in His *likeness*. Everyone is created in the *image* of God; if this were not so, we would not be human beings. Intrinsically speaking, a human being is a reflection of all the attributes of God in a single form, a form that is both spiritual and material, which is why we are commanded to act as God's steward on earth, and have the power to obey that command. But not everyone is in the *likeness* of God. If we are eaten up by sin, passion and ignorance, we are like a mirror that can no longer reflect the Sun's light because it is encrusted with mud. The mirror is intact and unbroken. But because of the filth that hides it, it can never do what it was designed to do. The human spirit—and to a certain degree, even the human body—are created in God's image. But the human soul must become obedient to, and pattern itself after, that image, so that the human being may be in God's *likeness* as well as in His image. Once the soul has come into the likeness of God, once it has gone through purgation and purification, once the mirror has been washed clean, then image of God can be clearly reflected in it; this is the real meaning of "my soul doth magnify the Lord."

The spiritual Path is the path of purgation, of purification. As we travel along this path, we move out of the state of fallen human nature, of original sin, and toward the state of "be ye perfect, even as your Heavenly Father is perfect." The Evangelical Protestants are right that we cannot follow this path by our own efforts. How can a fallen and corrupted human nature perfect itself? Every attempt by the corrupted soul to purify itself necessarily takes part in that corruption; there is no way we can "pull ourselves up by our own bootstraps." This is why we need God's freely-given grace, and the faith to receive it. For Christians, the only channel of God's grace is Jesus Christ, crucified and resurrected; for other religions, God has provided other channels, which are outwardly distinct from Christ, but inwardly one with Who Christ really is: the uncreated Logos, the Eternal Word of God.

Yet "works" too are part of the spiritual Path; the Catholics and the Eastern Orthodox Christians have always taught this. When the Protestant reformers, like Luther, taught that we are saved by "grace alone, through faith," besides protesting against Catholic abuses, such as the claim that it might be possible to buy an easier afterlife for gold and silver, I believe they were also reacting against the idea that "God does 50%, but we have to do the other 50%." That's absurd: God does 100% because He *is* 100%. How could He do any less? But still, we have to avail ourselves of that 100%. When Jesus said "be of good cheer, I have overcome the world," He was saying that God, through him, had already provided 100% of what we need. But when He said "take up your cross and follow Me," He was talking about *work*—backbreaking work, the kind of work that would be impossible for us without God's constant guidance and help. And yet, because of that freely-given and merciful help, "My yoke is easy and My burden light."

There is a Russian fairy tale that goes like this: Once there were three brothers who were the laziest men in the world. They refused to work for their daily bread, and so (not surprisingly) they ended up pretty hungry. One day they came upon an apple tree, but could not imagine climbing the tree to pick the apples, or even shaking the branches. Then one brother had an idea: "If we lie on our backs under the tree with our mouths open, surely apples will eventually fall into our mouths, won't they?" So that's what they did. After lying there for several hours, however, a second brother began to have misgivings: "But even after the apples fall into our mouths, we'll still have to *chew* them, won't we?" That's when the brothers realized that their plans had been over-ambitious. Disappointed, the three stood up and walked sadly away from the apple tree. Which is to say: the full and balanced assimilation of God's freely-given grace demands spiritual labor. Only God can open the prison gates, but we have to be willing to walk through them. *Receptivity requires sacrifice.* It takes real spiritual work to give up the idea that we can save ourselves by our own efforts, and to rely on God alone.

So the spiritual Path is a journey from our sinful and fallen selves to the perfection God has in store for us—from what we have made of ourselves, by our own efforts, in time, to the form in which God has created us, from all eternity. God creates us perfect; there can be no flaw in His work. And if that perfect image of us did not still exist in the mind of God, no matter how far we have fallen away from it, there is no way we could ever be restored to that perfection.

Like the Zen people say, "in order to be enlightened, first you have to be enlightened." Or like the character of "Dante" says in Dante's *Purgatorio*, "[to] return again / to where I am, I journey thus. . . ."

The idea of life as a journey from birth to death is commonplace, and people of religious faith, who believe in an eternal afterlife with God, will see the end of that journey—if they don't lose their way, that is, and wander off the true path—as heaven. The traditional spiritual ballad "I Am a Poor Wayfaring Stranger" perfectly expresses this idea. But songs like "Great High Mountain" (as sung by Ralph Stanley) and spirituals like "Ma Journey" (as sung by Marian Anderson) add another dimension: the idea—clearly implied rather than openly stated—that we may not have to wait until we die to see God, that we can reach Him in this life, through walking the spiritual Path. As it says in "Ma Journey":

> On ma journey now, Mount Zion
> On my journey now, Mount Zion
> O I wouldn't give nothin', Mount Zion
> For ma journey now, Mount Zion

The "journey" here is clearly not just the journey through life, but the spiritual Path. The world tempts the singer to sell the sovereign good of the Path, "the Pearl of great price," for the goods of this world, mere "fortunate" circumstances, but the singer refuses. She knows that no amount of security, pleasure or power, in worldly terms, can equal the Pearl, and that the Path stretches not simply through the circumstances of life, which on their own amount to little more than "one damn thing after another," but up the slopes of Mount Zion, the Mount of Purgatory, the way of self-purification, and ultimately self-annihilation in God.

The Path is something other than simply our day-to-day lives, even when lived in hope of heaven. It has real and discrete stages to it, milestones, signposts, even vehicles to travel in. But if we walk the spiritual Path with faith, zeal and constancy, in response to true spiritual guidance, then the day may come when our journey in the Spirit and the whole journey of our life turn out to be one and the same thing. This unity between the spiritual life and life in its totality is expressed in the traditional spiritual "King Jesus":

I was but young when I begun
No man can hinder me
But now my race is almost done
No man can hinder me.

Ride on, King Jesus
No man can hinder me;
Ride on, King Jesus, ride on
No man can hinder me.

PRIDE AND HUMILITY

Back when I attended Catholic high school in California in the 1960's—that was when the Catholic Church was still Catholic, and before high schools had turned into minimum security prisons—one of my teachers, Fr. Lacey, said something that I never forgot: "True pride and true humility are the same thing." Imagine hearing that from a high school teacher! Only somebody who had graduated from a truly *high* school could have transmitted a teaching like that. Later in life I heard the same thing again, in the words of a Sufi poet: "Everyone is proud of someone/And we are proud of God!"

Traditional English, Irish, Scottish, and Appalachian ballads often show this kind of pride, a pride that could only have originated in a caste of ancient warriors. The Bedouin Arabs and the Native Americans traditionally exhibited the same brand of warrior pride, a sense of honor which is inseparable from the humility demanded of all of us in the moment of facing death; as the Lakota say, "It is a good day to die." A warrior—especially in the days before war was mechanized, or under similar circumstances today—needs a military élan, like the "battle fury" of the Irish hero Cuchulainn; without the glory of war—the bright uniforms, the songs, martial music, the war-cry itself—who could face not only the terror but the *humiliation* of death, or of a long life lived to its end in silent suffering, without legs, without an arm, without a face? Rama Coomaraswamy (son of Ananda K. Coomaraswamy), a traditional Catholic who was initiated as a Hindu *brahmin* in his youth, once told me that just as the *brahmins*, the priestly caste, were saved from the spiritual pride of their high station by having to beg for their living from the *vaishyas*, the hard-headed, money-making solid citizens, so the *kshatriyas*, the warrior caste, were saved from the negative effects of warrior pride through the ever-present spectre of mutilation and death. Pride is only *true* when it is pride in something greater than oneself, something that one is privileged to serve and in the name of which one may even be granted the great honor of dying. That is the indissoluble bond, the blood-brothership, between pride and humility. The spiritual Path itself is often compared to warfare, which is why St. Paul said "I have fought the good fight," and why the Muslims call it "the greater *jihad*," the war against the passions. If one's honor attaches only to one's ego, then it is nothing but vanity, and is truly "in vain"—useless. But if one's honor resides in one's regiment, one's liege, one's nation, one's religion, one's lady, and ultimately in one's God, then that is true honor. From the spiritual standpoint, though not necessarily from the socio-historical one, "He who exalts himself shall be humbled," is vanity, while "He who humbles himself shall be exalted" is honor.

The Spanish have a concept known as *duende*, which comes from the phrase *duen de la casa*, "lord of the house." In folklore the *duende* is thought of as a kind of elf or household spirit, but there is every indication that it originally referred to God Himself, given that, to the Muslims who controlled and settled Spain for 800 years, "the House" is the Kaaba in Mecca, and "the Lord of the House" is Allah. The *duende* is the grim, passionate and beautiful power which makes a great warrior, a great bullfighter, a great singer, a great poet. (William James called for a "moral equivalent to war," to which I once replied—in that time of my life when I was deep in the throes of lyric inspiration, which included a taste for good Spanish sherry—"poetry is the moral equivalent of human sacrifice," an apparently extreme view which will appear less so to anyone who reflects on how many poets end by taking their own lives, as did my own poetic mentor, Beat Generation poet Lew Welch.) Thus the *duende* would correspond particularly to the Rigor and Majesty of God—*al-Jalal*, in Arabic—as opposed to (though also mysteriously at one with) the Mercy and Beauty of God, *al-Jamal*.

The great Spanish poet Federico García Lorca wrote an essay

called *The Duende: Theory and Divertissement.* In it he says, quoting Manuel Torres: "Whatever has black sounds, has *duende,*" and further: "The *Duende* ... will not approach at all if he does not see the possibility of death, if he is not convinced he will circle death's house. ..." This quality seems poles apart from the high angelic clarity and full-on sweetness of the Northern European soul, the Anglo-Celtic soul at its best, the quality so unmistakably carried in the voices of Jean Ritchie or the Carter Family (this being the very quality that makes the whitest of the White Race so terrible and inexorable when that angelic soul goes wrong). And yet, what else but Lorca's *duende*, with its "black sounds," drives through the voice of Ralph Stanley when he sings "O Death"?

Lorca quotes the following early Spanish folk song as an example of a wound dealt by the *duende*:

> Inside the garden
> I shall surely die.
> Inside the rosebush
> They will kill me.
> Mother, Mother, I went out
> Gathering roses,
> But surely death will find me
> In the garden.
> Mother, Mother, I went out
> Cutting roses,
> But surely death will find me
> In the rosebush.
> Inside the garden
> I shall surely die.
> In the rosebush
> They will kill me.

He also quotes a poem apparently both by and about the woman poet La Marabella of the 1600's, who, dying in childbirth by the roadside, says:

> The blood of my entrails
> Covers the horse,

And the horse's hooves
Strike fire from the pitch.

And beyond the obvious differences, can't we discern a quite similar spirit in "The Banks of the Ohio," or "Fair Margaret and Sweet William," or "Silver Dagger"? And in the traditional ballad "Matty Groves," the *duende* of the aristocratic warrior spirit is even more clearly present: Lord Darnell (in other versions, Lord Arnol), after catching Matty Groves in bed with his wife, says:

It's true I have two beaten swords
    And they cost me deep in the purse.
You shall have the better of them
    And I shall have the worse.
And you will strike the very first blow
    And strike it like a man;
I will strike the very next blow
    And I'll kill you if I can.

And, after beheading his wife (or, in another version, striking her though the heart and pinning her against the wall):

A grave, a grave! Lord Darnell cried
    To put these lovers in:
But bury my lady at the top,
    For she was of noble kin.

The Spanish, honor-ridden and enamoured of death though they be (or were; they're getting pretty "Euro" these days), have nothing on Scottish or border ballads like this, when it comes to *duende*. The *duende* is an essentially aristocratic emotion or force—and yet, as purely aristocratic mores died out in the west, at least within the confines of the class that produced them, they stepped down the ladder of the castes and, to a degree at least, became democratized. When a 19th-century man fought a duel, whatever his social class may have been, he was in one sense acting as a lord. Honor in the Middle Ages was an entirely aristocratic virtue, and only aristocrats were privileged to carry arms for their own purposes. And for the most part, only aristocrats rode horses, which means that, at least from the strictly traditional point of view, any armed rider was half a lord or half a knight, like John Hunt Morgan and his men, or Nathan Bedford Forrest—not to mention that terrible, blue-eyed, avenging angel, Stonewall Jackson. These were true American *kshatriyas*. U.S. Grant, on the other hand, was a pure *vaishya*, a stolid (and unsuccessful) storekeeper, unwilling herald of the more cynical, arrogant and successful Yankee robber barons of the Gilded Age, who kept all their honor in their purse. For all the "knightliness" of the Southern gentleman or military man, however, we must not forget that, in historical terms, the medieval knight—his supposed model—was always somewhere on a scale between chivalrous gentleman and armed thug. (Forrest, we should remember—the greatest American guerrilla warrior outside Geronimo—founded the infamous Ku Klux Klan). Still, when an Appalachian mountaineer swore to stand by his word, defend his land and his family against all comers, personally avenge his dead, and ask charity of no man, these were strictly aristocratic virtues, though the man bearing them might be among the poorest citizens of this nation. The only truly romantic nobility is disinherited nobility after all, as any Jacobite could tell you.

But what relationship, if any, does aristocracy have to the spiritual Path? Aristocrats are not more notoriously saintly than other people; their notoriety usually stems from a different quarter. Perhaps it has something to do with the saying of the great Christian sage Meister Eckhart (the greatest of all in the West, outside Dante): "The soul is an aristocrat." There is something unique and sovereign in the heart of every one of us, a thing of rare *quality* (as the aristocracy used to be called "the quality") rather than democratic *quantity*. As romantic love is reserved for "the One and Only," so the aristocracy of the soul—potentially, of *every* soul—is kin by blood (speaking here in strictly Christian terms) to that great King whose shed blood made His every follower His heir: in the words of St. Paul, "it is not I who live, but Christ lives in me." Whoever swears allegiance to the King of his Heart is an aristocrat, whatever his or her social position, while whoever takes the World as his boss, and the tyranny of public opinion, is trash at worst, and at best—a politician.

THE LANGUAGE OF ROMANCE AND METAPHYSICS

Once upon a time there existed a formal language of romance, certain elements of which were shared by a culture that stretched from Spain to Japan. It embraced the poems and ballads of Spanish poets and singers, both Muslim and Christian, the songs of the troubadours, the minnesingers and the meistersingers, the Arthurian romances of Britain, France and Germany, the lyrics and romances of Arabic and Persian poets, including Ibn al-ʿArabi, Jami, Nizami and Hafiz, the Sahaja poets of India like Chandidas and Kalidasa who wrote of the love of Krishna and Radha, the Shaivite poets who addressed their poems to Shiva and his Shakti, and Lady Murasaki's *Tale of Genji*. Shakespeare's sonnets were part of it, as well as the poetry of Donne and other Elizabethans. And the highest expression of it, in the West, was Dante's *Divine Comedy* and his *La Vita Nuova*. "Murasaki" means "purple" in Japanese—immediately suggesting the *murex* shells of the Mediterranean from which the famous Tyrian purple dye was derived. And Lady Murasaki was born in AD 973… yes, it was in many ways a single, nearly global culture. The shortest and most concentrated expression I have ever encountered of the spirit that animated it is the following *rubaʿi* (quatrain) by the Andalusian poet Ibn al-Qabturnuh (in Lysander Kemp's translation):

> I remembered Sulayma when the passion
>   of battle was as fierce
> As the passion of my body when we parted.
>
> I thought I saw, among the lances, the tall
>   perfection of her body,
> And when they bent toward me I embraced them.

Writers in this tradition dealt with love between human beings, but they also understood how human love could be a telling metaphor for the relationship between the soul and God. The sense of the sacredness of romantic attraction which they expressed came down to us in the form of poems; folk songs; popular love magic; children's rhyming games where little girls, jumping rope, used to practice an ancient form of divination to discover the name of their true love to be; and a profound cultural ethos that—along with the transmission of children's games via oral tradition from generation to generation, and various romantic superstitions and expectations held and practiced by adults—died in my lifetime. *She loves me; she loves me not.*

Consequently, we no longer know what men and women *are.* When hurricanes were named after women only, this represented a knowledge that stretched back to the beginning of the human race, a knowledge the Hindus designate by the word *Shakti*: the feminine, self-manifesting power of the Transcendent God. (The Hebrew *Shekhina*, the glory of God as revealed in the tent of the Tabernacle or the Temple at Jerusalem, carries the same basic idea, and is probably etymologically related.) Power appears in the form of vibration: light, sound, the waves of the sea, the cloud ripples in a mackerel sky. And so does *Shakti*. Every god in the Hindu pantheon (as well as the Egyptian and the Greek ones, and many others, under different names) was paired with his *Shakti*, his female consort. The English word "wife" is cognate with the word "vibrate, vibration," with the German *weib* (woman), and also with "wave"—a word-study that led the poet Gary Snyder to compose the following lines, from his poem "Regarding Wave":

> The Voice
> is a Wife
> to
>
>
> him still.

The poet is saying that the vibratory power of the human voice bears the same relationship to the body of the speaker as a god's *Shakti* bears to the god. *Still,* here, means both "even now" and also "motionless": the god, in the Hindu *tantra*, is motionless and impassive, even in the sexual act; it is his Wife, his Wave, his Power, who does all the dancing. A hurricane, then, is strictly analogous to, and a clear symbol of, the Spirit of God moving upon the face of the waters; it is literally the *Shakti*, the manifest power, of the Sun and his heat.

But now we have things like "Hurricane Larry": In the name of a meaningless and childish idea of "sexual equality," as well as a fear of anything even remotely suggesting romantic heterosexual love, we have unknowingly destroyed a profound symbol-system stretching back to the dawn of human history. And this is exactly what is to be expected at the tail-end of the Kali-Yuga: as polarity is the principle of cosmic manifestation, so the destruction of polarity is a clear sign of the *pralaya*, the dissolution of the manifest world.

FROM DUE WEST TO TRUE NORTH: A CRITIQUE OF PURE NOSTALGIA

There is something strangely nostalgic about this mysterious ground upon which we walk, a ground called America—something both more glamorous (if not glitzy) and more prosaic (if not bathetic) than anything Europe could produce. The ancient Irish aires looked west, in a heartrending, almost lethal nostalgia, toward the True West, the fortunate isles, the land beyond the sunset, to which St. Brendan voyaged and set mortal foot upon, never to return. The west was death, and memory—perhaps even the memory of the lost Atlantis. But to those Irish, and Scotch-Irish, and those Welsh, who actually sailed here—leaving behind them ballads of parting and heartbreak—that bloody nostalgia was softened somehow; because those who had traveled to this most alien of lands had also, mysteriously, come home. The West had been won. The land of the future has been conquered and held. And yet… there was something a bit posthumous about it, after all. Nobody standing on the California coast at sunset, looking out to the Farralones (those barren, rocky, bird-limed crags that I always liked to think of as the "Far Alones," the California version of Skellig Michael), could quite feel what an ancient Irish warrior or farmer or monk could feel looking west across the Atlantic. To him, the great Lost Land might yet be found again, if the Ocean were to be miraculously transformed into a flowering meadow under the wheels of Mananan MacLer's chariot, if St. Brendan could show the way—but what, after the west was won, was left for Americans to discover? What magic land beyond the sea—Vietnam? (Consult Herman Melville, in *Moby Dick*, for the answer to that one.) Walt Whitman wrote "Passage to India," but that early advertisement for globalism was ultimately more suited to astronauts, or astro-tourists, than traditional mythic travelers:

> Lo, soul! seest thou not God's purpose from the first?
> The earth to be spanned, connected by net-work,
> The people to become brothers and sisters. . . .
> The lands to be welded together. . . .
> Passage to more than India!. . . .
> O sun and moon, and all you stars! Sirius and Jupiter!
> Passage to you!

And Harte Crane's alcohol-fuelled Pacific romanticism, in sections of "The Bridge," was too airy to be truly nostalgic; when it came time to do himself in, he chose the Caribbean instead. Americans had already "arrived." They were home now, even *down* home. In these hills the blade-like battle-fury of the Irish aires—the chip on the shoulder of so many of those ballads, where beauty, as with the Spanish *duende,* is always wedded to violent death—became softened, homely, a bit more democratically sentimental (to follow the typology of W.B. Yeats from his great "channeled" text, *A Vision*) than aristocratically passionate. Yet that aristocratic passion was still there, under the surface. Where Yeats could quote the epitaph from an ancestor's gravestone in Drumcliff churchyard, "Cast a cold eye / On life, on death / Horseman, / Pass by," Jean Ritchie could still sing "Fair Nottamun Town," or Johnny Cash, "When the Man Comes Around" (or Bob Dylan, "All Along the Watchtower"; or Richard Fariña, "Children of Darkness.")

Nostalgia essentially looks West, toward the sunset. But the spiritual Path, the road to Heaven, looks to the North instead. (This will be fully explained a little further on, when we come to the exegesis of "Lady Gay.") The nostalgia of "westering" has a drunken quality to it; the Irish pickled it long ago at Old Bushmill's, the oldest distillery in the world, in *uisge beatha*, claimed to be the Water of Life (in the same sense that blood is "life" when spilled on the pavement)—but spiritual Path is sober: it's hard to be nostalgic about all those ice-bergs, those northern lights. Nostalgia may lead us to war, but the rigor of battle, when actually met, leaves no room for it. Yet within the cold, lucid crystal of that sobriety lives a drunkenness higher and purer than any worldly nostalgia; as I wrote one time, when I first formally embarked on the spiritual Path, and gave up drinking: "Better the wine of the desert than the desert born of wine."

The Hindus have a doctrine of the "two paths," the *pitri-yana* and the *deva-yana*. The *pitri-yana* is the path of the ancestors (literally the "way of the fathers"); the *deva-yana* is the path of the gods. The first leads to rebirth, the second to liberation. Nostalgia directs us to *pitri-yana*; nostalgia for the ancestors, for the old folks at home, draws us into the womb of becoming; we emerge as a baby, red-faced and squalling: *Fooled again!* In order to take the upward path, the path of the gods, we need to lay nostalgia out on the table, and coldly cut its throat. When Alabama sings

> Song, song of the South
> Sweet potato pie and I shut my mouth
> Gone, gone with the wind
> There ain't nobody lookin' back again

—well then, *don't* look back. Why keep playing that same old tune over and over? Forget about getting them to carry you back to Old Virginie. Be done with nostalgia; remember eternity as present in this very moment. Take it like a man and get to work.

The *westerly* quality of nostalgia, of *pitri-yana*, is classically ex-pressed in the poem "The Song Mt. Tamalpais Sings" by Lew Welch, which is the key-note poem of Marin County, California, the place where I grew up, as well as being an early draft of a suicide note:

> *This is the last place. There is nowhere else to go.*

> Human movements,
>   But for a few,
> Are Westerly.
> Man follows the Sun.

This is the last place. There is nowhere else to go.

> Or follows what he thinks to be the
> movement of the Sun.
> It is hard to feel it, as a rider,
> on a spinning ball.

This is the last place. There is nowhere else to go.

> Centuries and hoards of us,
> From every quarter of the earth,
> Now piling up,
> And each wave going back
> To get some more.

This is the last place. There is nowhere else to go.

> "My face is the map of the Steppes,"
> she said, on this mountain, looking West.
>
> My blood set singing by it,
> to the old tunes,
> Irish, still,
> among these Oaks.

This is the last place. There is nowhere else to go.

> This is why
> once again we celebrate
> the great Spring Tides.
> Beaches are strewn again with Jasper
> Agate, and Jade.
> The Mussel-rock stands clear.

This is the last place. There is nowhere else to go.

> This is why
> once again we celebrate the
> headland's huge, cairn-studded, fall
> into the Sea.

This is the last place. There is nowhere else to go.

> For we have walked the jeweled beaches
> At the feet of the final cliffs
> of all Man's wanderings.

This is the last place.
There is nowhere else we need to go.

Conversely, the *northerly* quality of *deva-yana*, the spiritual Path, is expressed by Edgar Lee Masters in the poem "Elijah Browning" from *Spoon River Anthology*:

> . . . . a mist as from an iceberg
> Clouded my steps. I was cold and in pain.
> Then the sun streamed on me again. . . .
> . . . . And above me
> Was the soundless air, pierced by a cone of ice
> Over which hung a solitary star! . . .
> I touched the star
> With my outstretched hand.
> I vanished utterly.
> For the mountain delivers to Infinite Truth
> Whosoever touches the star!

(Compare this with Masters' great poem of the *pitri-yana*, expressing the nobility as well as the pathos of ancestral piety, the one entitled "William H. Herndon.") The mountain is the Mount of Purgatory, above which—even though it is first described as rising from the southern ocean—Dante in the *Divine Comedy* places the constellations of the Bears. And the star is the Pole Star, the "still point of the turning world" (in Eliot's phrase), which so many ancient civilizations saw as the doorway leading beyond the universe, beyond the cycles of time.

The same sense of the spiritual Path as cold, northerly and mountainous (North, of the four directions, being the one that most clearly symbolizes the vertical dimension) also appears in John Herrmann's song "Bow Down," which—to judge from the liner-notes to the CD where it appears, *Songs from the Mountain*—is at least partly inspired by the motion picture *Cold Mountain*, as well as the novel of the same name by Charles Frazier, about North Carolina in the Civil War days; at the beginning of the book Frazier quotes from Gary Snyder's rendition of the *Cold Mountain Poems* by the Buddhist hermit-sage Han Shan, whose name means "Cold Mountain." Here's one of them:

> Clambering up the Cold Mountain path,
> The Cold Mountain trail goes on and on:
> The long gorge choked with scree and boulders,
> The wide creek, the mist blurred grass.
> The moss is slippery, though there's been no rain
> The pine sings, but there's no wind.
> Who can leap the world's ties
> And sit with me among the white clouds?

And some of John Herrmann's lyrics to "Bow Down," which are *right* enough to even deserve anonymity, go like this:

> All around the mountain it was so cold
> Couldn't hear nothing but the big wheel roll
> *Bow down*
> . . . .
> Wind blew north, wind blew south
> Wind blew sand in the black snake's mouth
> *Bow down*
> . . . .
> Wind blew up, wind blew back
> Wind blew snow in the fox's track
> *Bow down*

Note how "north and south" turns into "up and back"; the vertical dimension, signature of eternity, is clearly established here. The big wheel is the wheel of existence, whose visible sign is the wheel of the turning stars; the sound of its turning is "the music of the spheres." The wind is the Spirit, the Tao; when the Spirit stands up and moves, *bow down* is the only appropriate response. The wind chokes the black snake, stifles the passions. The cold wind hides the sage's footprints (the fox is the sage, Gurdjieff's "cunning man") under a seamless blanket of snow, because his is the *pathless path*. Neither Herrmann nor Han Shan are infected by nostalgia; they are looking North, not West.

Stephen Foster's "My Old Kentucky Home," on the other hand, is (like "The Song Mt. Tamalpais Sings") entirely Western. The theme of the song is a sort of *nostalgia for the present.* "We will sing one song / For the Old Kentucky Home / For the Old Kentucky Home far away," sings the old slave; he sings it even before he has actually left. When worldly nostalgia conquers and alienates us, we capitulate to time itself. With no sense of eternity remaining, *presence* becomes diffuse, till even the hand held directly before the face is "far away"; you can see the horizon right through the bones. *Remember earthly life? that bright and wavering dream? Why, here it is even now, all about us.* As the quintessential song of nostalgia for the (departed) present, "My Old Kentucky Home" accurately captures part of the felt quality of the land we Americans had arrived at when the country was first definitively settled, before the Civil War. We had actually come to the place Europe had longed for: El Dorado; the Seven Cities of Cibola; the Fountain of Youth. But all these places had looked much more glamorous, somehow, from that great Atlantic distance. Seen up close, the Seven Cities were mud villages; the Fountain of Youth was a Florida retirement community; and El Dorado—at least after the Gold Rush ended—was Hollywood. (The true City of Gold is the Heavenly Jerusalem. As Edgar Allen Poe said—the poet who first uncovered the truly *putrescent* quality of a nostalgia fuelled by spiritual despair: "Ride, boldly ride / The Shade replied / If you seek for El Dorado." As an alcoholic and opium addict, he knew too well that you couldn't get there by "laying back"—and, consequently, that he himself would never get there.)

Even though the slave in "My Old Kentucky Home" is being sold South, down the river, in mythic terms the song is pointed due West. It is pure nostalgia. There is no verticality, no eternity in it. It is entirely horizontal. But in "Hard Times," Foster's greatest song, the cry "Hard times, hard times, come again no more" begins to introduce a vertical element, since that cry is a cry for God's mercy, and mercy can only come *down* from above. (Like Marian Anderson sings in "Ma Journey": "One day, one day / I was walkin' along / When the elements opened/And the love come down.") A song like "Will the Circle Be Unbroken" is less nostalgic than "My Old Kentucky Home" because it is beginning to look to the next world, to eternity. In terms of compass-points, it is probably close to Northwest. And the songs "I'll Fly Away" and "Angel Band" are nearer to Northwest-and-by-North; in them, nostalgia has been almost entirely replaced by spiritual triumph. Death is swallowed up in Victory.

Because America is dying—or already dead, but as yet unaware of the fact—nostalgia has a peculiar function in our times. There is nothing more unsentimental and anti-nostalgic than "postmodern" technical culture, which has largely eaten up "modernist" literary culture everywhere (though New York still pretends otherwise); yet nostalgia may yet enlighten us as to exactly what we've lost. In a time when most of the United States has been sold to China by Wal-mart, and when our "stay the course" president has called up the last faint echoes of true American patriotism for use in the Iraq war, only to sell them on the cheap to the globalists—including the *Arab* globalists—along with much of our nation's sovereignty, perhaps we would do well to encounter again the two greatest dirges for America to be produced in the last twenty years: the magnificent Civil War TV series of Ken Burns, and the first concert in the series called *Down From the Mountain*. But to tell the truth, it was nostalgic all along; it was dying all along. The great, wide announcement of the American New Age, the American New Deal written by Walt Whitman was a farewell at the same time, a dirge from the very beginning: "Out of the Cradle Endlessly Rocking;" "When Lilacs Last in the Dooryard Bloomed"—it was poems like these that led D. H. Lawrence, in *Studies in Classic American Literature*, to call Whit-man the poet of death. What else could be expected, after all, from the poet laureate of the Land of Sunset? *Oh Shenandoah, I'm bound to leave you;* almost everybody wrote that song, or sang it, at one time or another. Everybody except maybe Emily Dickinson, who had some true northerly grit in her constitution, a real sense of the unsentimental rigors of the spiritual Path:

Far from love the Heavenly Father
  Leads the chosen child;
Oftener through realm of briar
  Than the meadow mild,

Oftener by the claw of dragon
  Than the hand of friend,
Leads the little one predestined
  To the native land.

Nostalgia ferries us across to the land of death, the realm of the ancestors, on a richly-appointed Egyptian barge. It does not carry us to heaven in a fiery chariot. So what, spiritually speaking, is the use of it? The use of nostalgia is to gather up the lost and scattered limbs of the soul, like Isis gathering the limbs of Osiris. Or rather, it is the quality that allows us to *find* those scattered members; the actual gathering up and stitching together, the true "re-membering," requires both our own sobriety and God's Grace and Power to accomplish. Nostalgia is always directed to what has been lost; it remembers the past and forgets eternity. The spiritual Path, on the other hand, remembers eternity, in which nothing is lost, or ever could be; and so the Path is without nostalgia. Nostalgia can recollect, up to a point, but it cannot purge—which is why the arc that sweeps from West to North must, at one point or another, pass through a region of profound psychic disgust.

The soul sunk in nostalgia has made a bad bargain, expressed succinctly in the song "Me and Bobbie McGee" (by Chris Christopherson) as: "I'd give all my tomorrows for a single yesterday." But the soul which has never felt nostalgia is in danger of living out its life ignorant of its own depths, oblivious to itself, on its own thin and brittle surface, in danger of never truly understanding how much it has lost, and coming to grips with that loss. Without nostalgia we can never realize that we are fallen, never believe in *original sin*. But without putting an end to nostalgia, we can never stand up again; take a stand; stand on our own two feet. The usual effect of an opening of the soul to deep, transpersonal nostalgias is for that soul to be swept away into the stream of temporality, the *pitri-yana*, the

River of Endless Farewell. But if one can hold fast to faith in God, to the concrete, spiritual present, and thus to eternity, while still remaining open to the immense vistas nostalgia has opened up—to all the lost souls, and everything that's lost in one's own soul—then the River reverses course, like the Mississippi did during that big earthquake on the New Madrid fault. Time no longer *passes*; time *arrives*. The River is now the path of the spawning salmon, fighting upstream, up the Mountain of Purgatory, to find and make new life.

This is what the Book of Revelations calls "the resurrection of the dead."

In sections III and IV above I have presented part of the cultural matrix, both ancient and contemporary, out of which the songs I will be explicating emerge to meet us. This treatment is preliminary to my main argument, and thus partly impressionistic. But don't be fooled: beyond this point, in the main body of the work, you will find (by and large) neither impressions nor musings, only pure science. Historical, social, cultural studies are the way of speculation and conjecture; the spiritual Path is the way of certainty. This is not to say that my interpretations are the only ones possible. True symbols bristle with meaning; they always mean more, much more, than all possible interpretations of them combined. But by the same token, these interpretations, when rightly informed, are not subjective impressions; they are soundings, taken from different latitudes and longitudes, of the true, objective depths of the Ocean we confront.

The Tibetans have a habit of hiding esoteric scriptures in caves or burying them in the earth, like the Dead Sea Scrolls. Then, maybe centuries later, somebody (called a *tertön*) appears who has had a dream or vision of exactly where these scriptures are hidden, and he goes and digs them up. This is one way that Tibetan Buddhism keeps itself fresh and alive: "familiarity breeds contempt" but "absence makes the heart grow fonder." As for myself, I believe I've had a vision, or at least half of one, of where a few such secrets lie buried in "the earth of song." I've got my pick, I've got my shovel, and I think I know where to dig; now let's see what I come up with.

I said above (didn't I?) that the world looks to be ending. But we must face the fact that it will most likely *never* end until all the secrets are told. So let's get to work and tell those secrets; it's a better course of action, in my opinion, than breeding the red heifer, and much less politically charged. In doing this we will be playing our own little part in the great work "turning the hearts of the fathers to the sons, and the sons to the fathers, before the great and terrible Day of the Lord."

1

LADY GAY

A MAP OF THE SPIRITUAL PATH

THE FOLK SONG "Lady Gay" is one version of "The Wife of Usher's Well," several variants of which were collected in Scotland and northern England by Francis James Child and in Appalachia by John Jacob Niles. When somebody who has studied traditional metaphysics looks at "Lady Gay," it shows itself to be a story of the spiritual Path, told in terms of the role of Nature—the *regime* of Nature—who wants to block our encounter with the Transcendent God, while actually working to prepare us for this very encounter. What Nature really *is*, is the visible manifestation of God in terms of signs and symbols. But when this truth is hidden, then Nature is no longer understood as *creation*, but appears as all-powerful and self-sufficient.

This version of "Lady Gay" is based on the one sung by Mason Brown and Chipper Thompson, which they believe "is traceable to Bascomb Lamar Lundsford . . . or it might be Buell Kazee," but "Ultimately, it all comes down to Pete Seeger anyway." To this version I have added three stanzas from two different versions of "The Wife of Usher's Well," from Child's collection (additions given in italics). If this approach opens me to the accusation of playing fast and loose with my material, picking and choosing only what will support my thesis, then I plead guilty. In 2005, when my wife and I were driving south from Lexington, Kentucky to Columbia, South Carolina to visit the wonder-working Sitka Icon of the Blessed Virgin which was touring the country (my wife is an Eastern Orthodox Christian), we were playing Brown and Thompson's CD *Born to*

Die—and I *heard* it. I heard what "Lady Gay" was all about. After that, it was easy to pick out which versions were true to the *real* song, and which ones were less so. It was a little like looking at photographs of someone you've known for years. "That one doesn't do her justice," you say; "but this one really captures her spirit." I believe that the grace of the Blessed Virgin, which was palpable to us during our trip to view her image, opened the meaning of the song to me. According to one Christian tradition, Eve, who became ugly through sin, was restored to beauty through the power of the Virgin Mary. Eve is the regime of fallen Nature, under which "all have sinned and come short of the glory of God"; the Virgin Mary is Nature redeemed, who says of herself, "behold the handmaid of the Lord; let it be done unto me according to Thy Word." So the Virgin taught us something about her sister on that trip. Lady Gay is Eve after she's washed off the dust and mud of the Fall and set herself up as a Great Goddess to rule the shattered universe, as if it weren't fallen at all, as if it were the most natural thing in the world.

This, I'm afraid, is how an unregenerate Platonist like myself will look at things: a thing most truly *is* in terms of its Idea, its eternal archetype; if you see a thing in light of its Idea, you see it whole. Everything else about that thing either conforms to the Idea, and so reveals it, or departs from that Idea, and so distorts and hides it. I fully realize that this is not the way folklorists, or scientists, or postmodern academicians, tend to look at things nowadays, but if my approach disqualifies me from accolades granted by the postmodernists (a distinction to which I do not aspire), it also disqualifies the postmodern nihilists from shooting me down: they can't draw a bead on me if they don't know where I'm coming from, if they can't see or imagine a place where things neither evolve nor decay or change over time—that Garden where all things simply *are*.

Let's travel through the song now, stanza by stanza:

> There was a lady, Lady Gay
>   Of children she had three
> Sent them away to the North Country [John Jacob Niles 33c
>   has "to a North Country priest"]
>   For to learn their grammaree

The word "gay" has many traditional reverberations. A peasant can be "merry," but only a great lady, a woman of independent means, can be "gay." The word suggests someone who is both care-free and wanton. Though the glossary in Child's collection gives its meaning as "beautiful," some etymologists derive it from a Frankish word meaning "impetuous." So the Lady Gay is clearly a "fast woman"; she is Queen Nature, whose powerful impulses command all who have not freed themselves from her; she is the Goddess of the Earth, the Great Mother *Gaia*.

As Robert Graves has demonstrated in *The White Goddess*, the Great Mother often appears in triple form, like the Furies or the Fates: she is Birth, Life and Death—the three dominant realities for anyone who thinks that this world is all there is, anyone who has lost the vision of the eternal, spiritual world. (And even to those of us who *can* see the spiritual world, the Goddess in her three forms is still tremendously compelling; according to God's will, she will test us to the bone.) So Lady Gay's "three sons" may have something to do with her triple nature; insofar as the Great Mother is a personification of primal Substance, the *Prakriti* of the Hindus, they certainly could symbolize the three modes of *Prakriti*: *sattwa* or purity, *rajas* or passion, and *tamas* or stagnation. But on another level, they also represent the three main "faculties" of the human soul: thought, will, and feeling. Feeling has most to do with birth, since in thoughtless sexuality we come close to acting on feeling alone, with immense consequences; will relates to the struggle of life; and thought, if we can truly *take* thought, shows us the uncertainty and brevity of life; it is the place of the *memento mori*. Also, will tends to develop later than feeling, and thought later than will. But these three faculties don't just relate to different phases of life; they are all a part of us now. And it is part of the science of the spiritual Path to teach us how to place these faculties in the right relationship with each other, so our soul can follow the will of God, praise Him, and finally *reflect* Him. If will follows feeling, we are wanton and dissipated, and the only thing we will use *thought* for is to scheme how to get what we want, regardless of the consequences, and then make excuses for all the damage we've done. If we want to be *upright* people, the will must place itself *below* thought, just as thought itself must be *under* the will of God, which is revealed to us both through scripture, and through the opening of the Eye of the Heart—the Transcendent Intellect within us that sees Truth just as directly and inevitably as the eye sees light. And if will follows true thought, then the feelings will follow too; we will not only *do* righteousness, we will *love* it. Our soul will *magnify the Lord.*

But what is the North Country? And what is this "grammaree"? In the hippy days, the received wisdom about these lines was that the North Country was Scotland, and "grammaree" was witchcraft, which was taught there, this idea being partly based this on those old books of magic spells called "grimoires." "You take the high road" says "The Bonnie Banks O' Loch Lomond," "and I'll take the low road, and I'll get to Scotland afore ye." Scotland also has associations with Freemasonry (as for example in the "Scottish Rite"), a tradition which retains at least a partial memory of the spiritual Path, and transmits some true lore about it. The suggestion here is perhaps that the three babes are being punished with death for the sin of practicing magic; yet the fact that the Niles version has "North Country priest" instead of just "North Country" suggests that they are after sacred knowledge, not just magical power— though there is also a definite anti-Papist ring to this stanza (at least to my ear), as if the course of study were not magic but priestcraft, and the sin being punished, intellectual pride.

There is undoubtedly some truth in all these different levels of understanding. But in terms of the spiritual Path, to learn one's "grammar" means much more than simply to practice magic; to work on one's "spelling" is something higher and greater than just learning to how cast spells. If we are going to understand the full significance of these lines, the rudimentary magical "Harry Potter" level of things will have to give way to the spiritual "Chronicles of Narnia" level. From the spiritual perspective, God is the One who uses a "grammar" of living symbolism to "compose" the universe. Magicians, and also those deviant Kabbalists who try to use the words of God in the Torah to write little scenarios of their own, think that *they* are the writers, that God's words in scripture and nature are simply there for them to use any way they want. (Plenty of scientists and engineers look at things the same way.) This is rather short-sighted, to say the least; it is short-sighted because such people don't really want to look down that long, lonesome road to see what the ultimate consequences of their frivolous meddling will be. The truth is, however, that only God is the Writer, and we—at our best—are like the parchment He writes on. If we can clear the pages of our Heart from all the doodles and scribblings put there by self-will and worldly experience, we will provide Him with a clean surface on which He can write His Own will for us, and the secrets of the universe, and finally His very own Name.

But what about the North Country? What is that, if it isn't Scotland? The North Country is the place of the Pole Star, that the poet T.S. Eliot called "the still point of the turning world," and which—symbolically speaking—is the gate to the higher spiritual realms. The whole night sky turns around that Star, but as for itself, it never moves. (This is probably where Aristotle got his idea that God is the "unmoved Mover.") If the universe is a *wheel* (the word *universe* means "one turn"), then the Pole Star is the *axel*. The North is the land called Hyperborea, which means "beyond the North Wind." The ancient Greeks had a legend of such a land, a place of eternal spring in the far North, which was where the sun-god Apollo came from; this probably had to do with poorly-understood reports of early explorers about the arctic summer, when the sun never sets. The Siberian shamans, the archaic Chinese, a lot of the Native Americans, and many other peoples see the North as the doorway to the Other World, and look at the Pole Star as the visible point of eternity in the created order. When the geese fly north for the summer they are returning to Hyperborea; in the winter they fly south again into this cramped and narrow stable we call earth. The Irish hear in the honking of the geese the barking of the Gabriel Hounds, who carry the souls of the dead to the next world. To the one who has come to the end of the spiritual Path, however, the border between this world and the next, at least in the inner dimension of things, is erased: as William Butler Yeats put it, in his poem *Byzantium*, "I call it death-in-life and life-in-death." The North Country is the land of the Transcendent God, the Father whom "no man hath seen . . . at any time" (John 1:18), who is totally beyond the visible, natural order of things. Ezekiel 8:3 speaks of the "inner gate [of the

Temple] that looketh toward the north, where was the seat of the image of jealousy, which provoketh to jealousy": the Transcendent God is a "jealous God" who "will have no strange gods before Him." He will allow no reality other than His Own to claim independent existence. But the realization of Transcendence doesn't happen all at once; if it did we could lose our minds from it, if it didn't kill us outright. The Great Mother Nature must prepare us for our encounter with the North Country. After schooling us in what are called the "lesser mysteries," she sends us off to Hyperborea to complete the "greater mysteries," which make up the post-graduate course.

The lesser mysteries have to do with reaching the "Earthly Paradise"—which is another way of saying that they teach us how to become true human beings. We humans are the only creatures created by God who have to work to become what we potentially already are. Animals are ruled by instinct; angels are each ruled by the single Idea they eternally contemplate and express; stars and galaxies follow natural law. Only human beings must struggle to attain their true place in the scheme of things. God gave human beings the whole spectrum of animal powers and desires, as well as a free will, a rational mind, and a Heart with an Eye in the center of it. In other words, He designed us to surpass ourselves. If we choose to follow what the Eye of the Heart shows us, as interpreted by the rational mind—and we will have to renew this choice every day of our lives—then we are on the way to becoming real human beings, thus completing the lesser mysteries, the first stretch of the spiritual Path. The lesser mysteries are a course which takes us back to the state Adam and Eve were in before they ate the fruit of the Tree of the Knowledge of Good and Evil, and lost their home in Eden. But if we choose instead to follow the animal powers of our soul, and use our will and rational mind to serve those powers, then we will fall below the human form. Somebody who is an alcoholic, or addicted to prescription pain killers, or sexually promiscuous, making babies right and left, or getting into unnecessary debt simply through carelessness, or always getting into fights, is—at least in a part of themselves—missing what it is to be a complete human being. The animal powers are not evil in themselves, but they do need to be tamed. In the Garden of Eden the animals did not prey upon each other, and after the Messiah comes "the lion will lay down with the lamb." Both of these conditions symbolize the state of the Earthly Paradise, which is the state we can live in while still in this world, if we come to place where all the animal powers of our soul obey us, just as we obey the Word of God.

That's the lesser mysteries. The greater mysteries have to do with the direct encounter with God, as when the Lord "spoke to Job out of the whirlwind." The lesser mysteries are for the most part moral and psychological; the greater mysteries are spiritual and mystical. Once our lives are balanced morally and socially and psychologically, then we can—if it is God's will for us, if we have both the call and the capacity to follow it—begin to know Him directly.

> They hadn't been there very long
>   Scarcely six months and a day
> When death, cold death came hastin' along
>   Stole them babies' lives away.

Six months indicates a 180-degree turn, what the Greek Bible calls a *metanoia*, which is a total change of mind—even a going beyond the mind entirely; many English Bibles translate *metanoia* as "repentance." Midwinter is six months from midsummer, and is the complete opposite of it. And the "death" that steals them babies' lives away is the death of the ego. The lore of the greater mysteries from many traditions routinely symbolizes, by the image of death, the self-transcendence whereby we encounter the Transcendent God. We die to all we know or remember or *believe* ourselves to be, and live on only as what God Himself *knows* us to be; so the spiritual death is also a death and resurrection. This is what is meant by Jesus' words, "He who seeks to keep his life shall lose it"—in the lower, sub-human worlds where the animal powers rule—"but he who loses his life, for My sake, shall find it."

> '*I wish the wind may never cease*
>   *Nor fashes* [troubles] *in the flood*
> *Till my three sons come hame to me*
>   *In earthly flesh and blood.*'
> [Child, "The Wife of Usher's Well," variant A]

Here the Great Goddess speaks in her own true voice. Other versions of "The Wife of Usher's Well" have the Wife or Lady praying to the Heavenly King for her sons' lives, but here she speaks a powerful magic spell on her own personal authority; she *curses her sons to live.* Speaking as Mother Nature, she calls for endless destructive winds and floods, or for an unending flood of troubles, until she can get possession of her sons again, who taken together are the human soul. Nature prepares us to go beyond her, to reach the higher spiritual worlds, and then doesn't want to let us go. If the wind of the Spirit (a word that literally means "breath" or "wind") could blow her sons away from her, then it can damn well blow them back again. This shows how, from Mother Nature's point of view, the Spirit is a wind that blows *inside* her, in a great circle, from life to death and from death back to life again. The idea that the Spirit of God could be *beyond* her, that there is something higher, more spiritual and more eternal than the great wheel of birth and death, is simply inconceivable to her. She is the whole show; she is the only game in town. From her narrow-minded, purblind viewpoint, there is no such thing as the Father, the Transcendent God.

> It was long 'round Martinmas
>   The nights being cold and clear
> She looked and seen her three little babes
>   Come a-runnin' on to her

Martinmas is November eleventh, in late Autumn—six months and a whole world away from the month of May, the month of the Roman Goddess Maia, who is *Maya*: the magical power that reveals God by weaving the world-illusion, and simultaneously hides Him behind the pattern that she weaves. Lady Gay occupies the merry month of May, the month of Taurus, the time of earthy wantonness and freedom from care, but her sons return to her from the direction of November, the month of Scorpio, the quarter of death. Transcendence now returns to encounter all it has transcended, which attempts to reassert its rights over that Transcendence; but this can never be.

> She set a table long and wide

And put on bread and wine
  Come eat, come drink you three little babes
  Come eat and drink of mine

Here the Lady concocts a false and contrary Eucharist to tempt her children to return to her. It is a common theme in mythology, as in the myth of Orpheus, that to eat the food of the underworld, the world of death, is to be trapped by that world—and to the three sons, who have realized a Life higher than the natural one, the world of Nature *is* the world of death. The bread and wine the Lady lays out for them are not the bread and wine of life, the body and blood of the Savior, but represent a false attempt on the part of the regime of Nature to appropriate the rights and powers that only the Divinity can truly possess. This is just what Maya does; she sets up a mirror to catch the light of God, and when we follow that light we move farther and farther away His true location. Whenever we believe that something in the world of the animal powers can give us real spiritual nourishment (the bread) or true spiritual insight (the wine), we have let ourselves be kidnapped and imprisoned by Lady Gay.

The bed was fixed in the back room
  On it was some clean white sheet
And on the top was a golden cloth
  To make those little babes sleep.

"Wake up! wake up!" says the oldest one
  "Wake up! it's almost day.
And to our Saviour we must return
  To-night or in the morning soon.'
  [Child, "The Wife of Usher's Well, variant D]

The most powerful magic Maya can weave to divert us from the spiritual Path and make us forget God is *sleep*—ignorance—that *lethal* spiritual complacency which hides, and also feeds upon, the fear of death; the "back room" here symbolizes the Unconscious, in the entirely negative sense of "everything we don't want to become conscious of." "Go to sleep ye little baby," sang the sirens in *O Brother Where Art Thou?* But the oldest son cries "sleepers, awake!"

Wakefulness is a universal symbol of spiritual knowledge; the word *Buddha* means "the one who woke up completely." The oldest son, here, is *thought.* Because thought comes last in our soul-development, we might tend to think of it as the youngest son, but it is actually the faculty of our maturity, and therefore the oldest. *Take thought*, it says; *remember the Path; remember that this world is not your home.*

> We want none of your bread, mother
>> Neither do we want your wine
> For yonder stands our Savior dear
>> And to Him we must resign

Awake, the three sons who are the human soul know that the World cannot provide the true sacrament of sanctification—only He who has overcome the World.

> Green ~~green~~ grass grows above [*our head*]
>> Cold clay at ~~her~~ [*our*] feet
> And every tear you shed for us
>> It wets our windin' sheet

Here the condition of the three babes in the grave is made to stand for the condition of all of us in this lower world where Death apparently rules; this is the only version of their "death" that the Lady Gay can believe in or understand. All of us, sojourners in this world, have the green grass of the Earthly Paradise growing over our head—which, if we can rise into the fullness of the human form, we can walk upon freely, like Adam and Eve when they "walked with God in the cool of the evening." And all of us have cold clay under our feet, which will smother and choke the life out of us if we sink into it—the clay of matter apparently bereft of the Spirit, and of the materialistic philosophies that rise like swamp-mist out of that darkened vision.

And the windin'-sheet? That's the fabric woven by Maya, the cloth we name "this World" and take to be the only reality—the same cloth that Ulysses' wife Penelope, in Homer's *Odyssey*, wove by day and unraveled again by night. While we are sunk in this world and dead to the Spirit, we exist like corpses wrapped in Maya's mummy-cloth. And the secret of Maya, the great Queen who seems so powerful, so self-sufficient, so carefree and gay, is that she does indeed weep. Somewhere she knows that she is nothing without the Father, that her destined lot is all the pain of birth and death, and the ignorance and the sleep that keeps the wheel of them ever turning. But just as the Hindus divide Maya into two aspects, into *avidya-maya* that hides the face of God and *vidya-maya* that reveals it, so the tears of the Great Mother are also of two kinds. One kind are the tears she weeps in despair of God—because if she is indeed the All-in-All, and suffering is not ended, what hope can she know? The other kind are the tears she weeps in repentance, in the realization that she is nothing in herself, that she is only the pattern of signs and symbols manifesting and praising the Invisible Father, the One God. The first tears are the ones that wet the cold clay that wants to drag us down into materialism, hopeless fatalism and spiritual despair; the second tears are the ones that water the green grass of Eden: to repent of the belief that you are self-created and self-sufficient—the root belief of the human ego—and to realize your total dependency upon the Creator, is to call down the Mercy of God, and walk alive into to Paradise. (In your Heart, at least. Even if you carry the true Philosopher's Stone in your pocket, life is still hard. The Stone doesn't make things easy, but it does teach you that "easy" isn't the be-all and end-all; it shows you how to turn *hard* into *true*.)

> Fare thee well, mother dear
>   Fare thee well, to barn and byre
> An' fare thee well, you pretty little gal
>   That tends our mother's fire.

Here the three sons make their final farewell to the natural order— and yet, who is that fire-tender, that pretty little gal? Why haven't we heard about her before? As soon as the Lady Gay is revealed as *avidya-maya*, as the natural order opposed to God and hiding His Face, the *spiritual essence* of the natural order, *vidya-maya*, is also revealed. The girl who tends the fire is the Goddess Vesta (Roman) or Hestia (Greek), the Goddess of the Hearth, who in Ireland appears as St. Bridgit of Kildare. (Plotinus identifies Hestia and her hearth with pure Being, the ultimate Origin of all things). She is the "domestic" side of Nature, the part that has to do with culture and cultivation, imitating and drawing upon Nature's order and balance. Nature is not a pure material chaos; she is also a Temple where the fire of the Spirit burns in secret, like the eternal flame tended by the Goddess Vesta's devotees, the Vestal Virgins. Just as we cannot walk the spiritual Path without the grace of the Transcendent God, so we cannot begin our spiritual journey until we also tap these *natural* potentials for *greater-than-natural* life through which Nature herself prepares us to go beyond her. The fire of the Spirit is hidden in the secret hearth of Nature until the Transcendent God is realized—but after He *is* realized, then traces of Him appear everywhere: Transcendence—the aspect of God that places Him beyond all we can see or know or feel or conceive—gives way to Immanence—the aspect of God whereby He lives in all things, is symbolized and indicated by all things.

Of the various ancient sacred sciences, the main science relating to the lesser mysteries is *alchemy*, whose patroness is Hestia (alchemy being a kind of culinary art, one in which the cook is also the meal), as well as the Eastern Orthodox saint, Mary of Egypt (who, according to legend, was supposed to have invented the cooking utensil known as the double boiler). Egypt is the material world, but St. Mary—though she was undoubtedly a real historical person—also represents that aspect of the Blessed Virgin that works in and through Nature, to spiritualize and redeem it. Alchemy is supposed to be a way to transmute base metals into gold, but when we understand it as a *spiritual* science, we realize that these "base metals" are really things that live in the human soul—*lead* being, let us say, a laziness that could be real substance; *iron*, a meanness and hard-heartedness that could be courage; *quicksilver*, a childish irresponsibility that could be true creativity, etc.—and that to say we must transmute these things into *gold* is simply to say, in metallurgical language, that we must become true human beings. Gold is precious not only because it is rare; it is also precious because it is beautiful, because it represents light made solid and dark matter made radiant—this being the "materialization of the spirit and spiritualization of the body" that produces the Philosopher's Stone, the human soul brought into light and order and stability under the rule of the Spirit. (The Philosopher's Stone is also a reflection, on the level of the lesser mysteries, of the Incarnation of Christ.)

So the pretty little gal that tends the Lady's fire is *vidya-maya*, the alchemical side of Nature that both prepares us for the spiritual Path and flowers into the full Immanence of God when the Path is complete. (Cooking, like farming and blacksmithing and carpentry and masonry, is essentially an alchemical art, since it works to "civilize" matter for human use.) The three sons say good-bye to her as they leave this world, but one wonders what may be the final outcome of this last look back. She *is* an awful pretty little gal; maybe some day they'll come back to take her with them—when the stars fall from heaven, and the powers of heaven are shaken.

2

PIRI-MIRI-
DICTUM DOMINI

ONE OF THE MOST COMMON and most obvious ways that hidden meanings are incorporated into folk songs appears in the genre knows as the "riddle song." We are used to thinking of a riddles as jokes, but earlier cultures used them as exercises to sharpen thinking and train intuition, as well as ways of transmitting esoteric secrets. (Sometimes jokes themselves can play the same role. The Muslim folkloric figure Mullah Nasruddin is the hero of many humorous stories that are sometimes used to transmit esoteric secrets by certain Sufi circles; at least one of Nasruddin's "routines" was later used by the Marx Brothers.) Some of the earliest Anglo-Saxon poetry is in the form of riddles; my own poetic mentor, Beat Generation poet Lew Welch, used riddles as teaching-tools. Another example of the use of riddles to stimulate spiritual insight is the Zen *koan*, such as "what is the sound of one hand clapping?"

The song "Piri-miri-dictum Domini" (Niles 1C), a variant of the riddle-song "I Gave My Love a Cherry," is clearly intended both to teach people how to think, and to present esoteric lore in concentrated form. The lyrics are a mixture of English and corrupt or imitation Latin, but even so, the song's original intent isn't too hard to make out.

> I had three cousins over the sea,
> *Piri-miri-dictum Domini.*

Three or four presents they sent to me,
Pantrum quartrum paradise stantrum,
Piri-miri-dictum Domini.

The first was a bird without a bone,
Piri-miri-dictum Domini.
The second was a cherry without a stone,
Pantrum quartrum paradise stantrum,
Piri-miri-dictum Domini.

The third was a book that no man's read,
Piri-miri-dictum Domini.
The fourth was a blanket without a thread,
Pantrum quartrum paradise stantrum,
Piri-miri-dictum Domini.

Can there be a bird without a bone?
Piri-miri-dictum Domini.
Can there be a cherry without a stone?
Pantrum quartrum paradise stantrum,
Piri-miri-dictum Domini.

A bird in the egg's without a bone,
Piri-miri-dictum Domini.
A cherry in the bud's without a stone,
Pantrum quartrum paradise stantrum,
Piri-miri-dictum Domini.

Can there be a book that no man's read?
Piri-miri-dictum Domini.
Can there be a blanket without a thread?
Pantrum quartrum paradise stantrum,
Piri-miri-dictum Domini.

A book in the press, that no man's read,
Piri-miri-dictum Domini.
A blanket in the wool's without a thread,
Pantrum quartrum paradise stantrum,
Piri-miri-dictum Domini.

The title alone indicates that the intent of the song is to teach spiritual truth. *Dictum Domini* means "word of the Lord" in Latin, and while *piri-miri* may be derived from some other Latin phrase, now corrupt and undecipherable, it is very interesting that *pir* means "elder" or "wise old man" in Persian, while *mir* means "chief" in the same language; both words are roughly similar in meaning to "lord," which is a title applied in many different languages to spiritual teachers. (*Piri* and *miri* would be the possessive forms of *pir* and *mir* when imported into Arabic.) When Jesus' disciples and others addressed him, they used the word *rabbi*, which, like the Arabic *rab*, can be adequately translated into English as "lord."

The basic message of "Piri-miri-dictum Domini" is *return to the Quintessence*, to the Formless. In terms of the spiritual Path, to become formless is to let God *recreate* or *reform* us. According to John 3:1–5,

> There was a man of the Pharisees, named Nicodemus, a ruler of the Jews: The same came to Jesus by night, and said unto him, Rabbi, we know that thou art a teacher come from God: for no man can do these miracles that thou doest, except God be with him. Jesus answered and said unto him, Verily, verily, I say unto thee, Except a man be born again, he cannot see the kingdom of God. Nicodemus saith unto him, How can a man be born when he is old? can he enter the second time into his mother's womb, and be born? Jesus answered, Verily, verily, I say unto thee, Except a man be born of water and the Spirit, he cannot enter into the kingdom of God.

In the practice of alchemy there are three main steps: *blackening*—dying to the "natural man," the "old Adam"; *whitening*—return to the perfect receptivity of the Formless; and *reddening*—receiving a new form by the power of the Spirit. "Piri-miri-dictum Domini" is about *whitening*; it has the same basic meaning as the Zen *koan* "show me your original face before you were born."

The song talks about four things (two natural, two man-made) from the standpoint not of their visible forms but of their formless essences: a cherry, a blanket, a bird and a book. When sets of four things appear in mythology, religious doctrine, songs or folktales they usually have something to do with what the Hindus and the Tibetan Buddhists call the *mandala*, whose simplest form is a cross inscribed inside a circle. *Mandalas* relate to the four seasons and the four directions; the Native American "medicine wheel" is one form of *mandala*. In alchemy, the most common *mandala* is based on the four elements: earth, water, air and fire. And the *quintessence* (which literally means "fifth essence") is the center-point of the *mandala* of the elements, the station of the Formless.

The cherry represents the *vegetable soul* (earth), which expresses itself through the automatic and mostly unconscious bodily functions. The lamb's-wool is the *animal soul* (water), which has to do with deliberate physical activity, and also the emotions. (Trees are rooted in the earth; animals are mostly water.) The bird is the *mental soul* (air) which rules thought. The association of birds with thought or intuition is common in folklore and colloquial speech. ("How do you know?" "A little bird told me.") And the book represents the spiritual Intellect which is higher than thought, the *intellectual soul* (fire) that reads the hidden Words of God. A cherry in the bud, a blanket before the wool is shorn and carded and spun and woven, a bird in the egg and a book that's still in press symbolize the state of these four souls, or of their archetypes, in that timeless time before the world was made, before you and I came out of our mother's womb, out of the place of "before Abraham came to be, I am." (In the riddle-song "I gave my Love a Cherry" [Niles 1 B], a variant of "Piri-miri-dictum Domini," we can see—cast into the form of a man's tender feelings for a beloved woman's pregnancy— this same sense of the Formless world: to intuit how we rise into human form out of that Formlessness is also to begin to get an inkling of the way back.) In the words of Psalm 104:29–30, if we can return to the place of "thou takest away their breath, they die, and return to their dust," then we can know the truth of "Thou sendest forth thy spirit, they are created: and thou renewest the face of the earth." So this song shows that we can't come into the place where God can renew our souls unless *all* parts of us—our body, our feelings, our thoughts, even our spiritual vision—are sacrificed to Him, as those of Jesus were sacrificed at his Baptism in the Jordan, and later—more completely—at his death on the Cross. Only then, like Jesus, can we be born again "of water and the Spirit."

But who are the "three cousins over the sea"? The sea is what separates this world from the next (like the sea the three sons sail over in "The Wife of Usher's Well"), so clearly the cousins have something to do with that world. They may be a kind of reflection of the Holy Trinity, but I believe that their main meaning is something different. That the gifts they send are "three *or* four" is a way of saying that the book, *the intellectual soul*, doesn't fully come into this world like the vegetable, animal and mental souls do; in a way it always remains in the other world, and stands as a doorway to that world. In the *I Ching* and many other sources, three is the number Heaven, as in the Holy Trinity, while four is the number of the Earth, as in the four directions, the four seasons etc.; thus to say "three or four" is to indicate an encounter, or interaction, between this world and the next. And just as three souls are sent and one remains, so three of the four cousins remain in the other world, while only one is sent to live here. This is a way of saying that the intellectual soul is predominant because it is closest to God; though it alone of the four souls remains partly in the other world, it carries with it three times the reality of all those three souls, taken together, that came fully into this world.

And what about the other mock-Latin line, "*Pantrum quartrum paradise stantrum*"? *Pantrum* suggests the Greek word *pan*, meaning "all"; *quartrum* is "quarter," *stantrum* just means "stand," in the sense of standing up, and also of standing still. And *paradise*—is Paradise. So here we have another song about the lesser mysteries that lead the human soul back to the Earthly Paradise; the line might be re-written: "When the All is quartered, Paradise is established." The quartering of the All, as when a cross is drawn on the earth for a medicine wheel, establishes the Center to which we return in the course of the lesser mysteries; the act of discriminating between the Four Elements or the Four Souls posits the Fifth element, the Quintessence. In practice, this means that we need to be able to tell the difference, in our own actual experience, between instinct, emotion, thought and Spiritual Knowledge; once we've done this, we are standing—virtually, at least—at the Absolute Center that transcends all of them. And once this Center is reached, we can rise to meet our God in the heavens above, this being the province of the greater mysteries. (In Genesis 2:10–14 this quartering is symbolized by the four rivers of Eden: the Pison, the Gion, the Hiddekel and the Euphrates.) On the night when the Prophet Muhammad ascended to heaven, he had to fly to the Center first, which was Jerusalem; only from Temple Mount, from the rock where Abraham was ordered by God to sacrifice his son, and where God's angel stayed his hand, could Muhammad rise into the spiritual worlds. As soon as we get a feeling for the reality of that Center, it begins to attract us like a magnet attracts iron; our four souls, the vegetable, the animal, the mental and the intellectual, change direction and begin to flow, like four living rivers, back to the quintessence, to the fifth element known as *aether*, to their original Source and Substance in the Formless World.

The great Hindu sage of modern times, Ramana Maharshi, taught a practice called "self-inquiry," based on the question "who am I?" The answers that spontaneously arise, if one asks this question deeply enough, are: "I am not the body; I am not the feelings; I am not the mind; I am not even the habit of saying 'I am' this or that thing, not even 'I am the Self.' I am indeed that very Self, the *Atman*, the Absolute Witness—God within us, in the act of seeing through our eyes—but I Am That without self-identification. The eye witnesses all things, but never witnesses itself as an object, because no eye can see itself, only its mirror-image—and the mirror-image is not the eye. The image of the eye in a mirror is merely one object among others; the true Eye that sees all, the true 'I' that knows Who He is purely by *being* Who He is, is forever unseen. When God spoke to Moses at the burning bush, He did not say "I Am" this or that; He said "*I Am That I Am.*"

"Piri-miri-dictum Domini" presents a preliminary approach to essentially the same practice.

3

FAIR NOTTAMUN TOWN

MYSTICAL AND ALCHEMICAL
SYMBOLISM IN AN APPALACHIAN FOLK SONG

ONE OF THE TRADEMARKS of traditional Appalachian folk singer Jean Ritchie is a song called "Fair Nottamun Town," which passed to her through her family. (Bob Dylan used the same tune for his song "Masters of War.") She tells how she and her sisters, as children, used to sit in the evenings on the porch of their farmhouse near the town of Hazard in Perry County, Kentucky, and try to untangle its meaning. In later years, on a trip to England, she learned that "Nottamun Town" is a version of the English mummer-song "Nottingham Town," and that the song has a taboo on it: whoever figures out its meaning will lose all of his or her luck.

The text of Jean Ritchie's version is as follows:

> In fair Nottamun Town, not a soul would look up
> Not a soul would look up, not a soul would look down
> Not a soul would look up, not a soul would look down
> To show me the way to fair Nottamun Town
>
> I rode a gray horse, a mule roany mare
> Gray mane and gray tail, green stripe down her back
> Gray mane and gray tail, green stripe down her back
> There wa'nt a hair on her be'what was coal black
>
> She stood so still she threw me to the dirt
> She tore-a my hide and bruis-ed my shirt
> From saddle to stirrup I mounted again
> And on my ten toes I rode over the plain.

Met the King and the Queen and a company more
A-ridin' behind and a-marchin' before
Come a stark-nekkid drummer a-beatin' a drum
With his hands in his bosom come marchin' along

They laughed and they smiled, not a soul did look gay
They talked all the while, not a word did they say
I bought me a quart to keep gladness away
And to stifle the dust, for it rained the whole day

Set down on a hard, hot cold-frozen stone
Ten-thousand stood around me, yet I'uz alone
Took my hat in my hands for to keep my head warm
Ten thousand got drownded that never was born
[*Fair Nottamun Town*, ©1964, 1979, Jean Ritchie, Geordie Music Publ. Co.]

The mummers were costumed actors who participated in midwinter festivals in ancient and medieval Europe, largely in pantomime, though songs also formed part of the performance. In the Middle Ages they performed at Christmas; the tradition of the Christmas-mummers in England was revived in perhaps the 18th century. Their plays included such motifs as the duel, death-and-resurrection, and the triumph of St. George over the dragon. The word "mummer," possibly derived from the Greek word for "mask," is related to the English word "mum"; to "keep mum" means "to act like a mummer, a mime"—though the word "mime" comes from the Greek *mimesis*, "imitation; art," which is related to the Sanskrit *maya*, the magical or dramatic power by which the Absolute manifests Itself as the universe. The universe, like a *mask*, both veils and reveals the *mystery* of the Absolute Reality. The symbolism found in "Nottamun Town" also suggests that the mummers, at one point in their history, may have had some relation to the tradition of Christian Hermeticism.

It is interesting, however, that the first two lines of stanza five, perfectly accurate in their context and entirely at one with the genius of the song, were written by Jean Ritchie herself (she tells me), following a vision she had, while walking in the woods, of the procession that appears in that stanza—proving that the ancient but always-new lore of the Primordial Tradition is transmitted by inspiration as well as memory, even if the one inspired is not entirely certain about, or necessarily even interested in, the *intellectual* meaning of the gift he or she has been given. So René Guénon's idea that the folk act as no more than a passive receptacle for metaphysical ideas received and transmitted by the esoteric sages must clearly be supplemented by the understanding that "the Spirit bloweth where it listeth," that artists working consciously within folk traditions can sometimes be inspired by the same Source that the sage himself also acknowledges and serves; no-one can put their copyright on Wisdom, or their brand on Truth.

In traditional cultures, silence, like any essential human gesture, is not neutral. It indicates not simply the subjective desire not to speak, but the objective presence of a "mystery," an initiatory secret; the Greek word for "mystery," *mysterion*, is closely related to the verb *myo*, which means "to shut the mouth," to "keep mum." And to judge from "Nottamun Town," the silence of the mummers was symbolic in precisely this sense, indicating that they were the transmitters, perhaps at one time the conscious transmitters, of mystical or alchemical lore in cryptic form.

In any fully traditional culture there is always a give-and-take between initiatory mysteries on the one hand and popular religion and/or folklore on the other, whether or not this exchange is mediated by an established "church." To take only one example, the Hindu *Mahabharata* may be viewed either as a mass of folklore which has collected around the core of a sophisticated literary epic, consciously designed to transmit a mystical doctrine in the guise of a semi-historical legend, or as a consciously-composed mystical epic which has drawn on a mass of mystical and/or historical folklore for its raw material. This ambiguity and tension between the two poles of aristocratic literature and folk legend is expressed in the epic itself through the figure of the sage Vyasa, who is at once the poet who composed the *Mahabharata* and a character appearing within it. And this two-way flow of lore between the folk and the literati seems to have taken place in the mummer-tradition as well, where established poets would compose libretti for mummer-plays based on folk material—literary ballads which, after a generation or two, might themselves be transformed into folk songs.

The mystical truth which is realized in the sage is virtual in the folk. If the folk are the field, the sage is the fruit of the tree which grows in the center of it, a fruit which, even as it takes its place in the eternal domain of God's attributes, also cyclically returns to the field from which it grew, via its seed, to propagate wisdom. The folk correspond to the Aristotelian *materia*, that which receives the imprint of forms, and the sage to *forma*, that which shapes or "informs" the material which allows it to appear. And the tree corresponds to Tradition in the sense employed by French metaphysician René Guénon: that body of spiritual Truth, lying at the core of every religious revelation and a great deal of folklore and mythology, which has always been known by the "gnostics" of the race since it is eternal in relation to human time, representing as it does the eternal design or prototype of Humanity itself. A traditional culture permeated by half-understood mystical lore on the folk level is a fertile matrix for the full development of the gnostic, the sagacious individual, who, by means of his *darshan*, his willingness to allow himself to be contemplated as a representative of spiritual Truth, returns the seed of wisdom to the folk who venerate him. Such a sage may also compose tales, ballads, riddles, plays, proverbs, and dances impregnated with mystical lore rendered into cryptic form, which can be subconsciously assimilated by the folk without breaking the seal of the mysteries. A great deal of Sufi lore, for example, has been transmitted in this way. And if mystical truths may be shown to ordinary people in dreams—who will be unable to consciously understand and assimilate these truths in the absence of a traditional hermeneutic and a mystagogue who can employ it, unless God wills otherwise—then we can also say that there is a constant two-way communication between the enlightened sage and the people via the subtle realm, or between God and the people via the sage—a communication which, however, only the sage is fully conscious of. The voice of the people may be the Voice of God—*vox populi vox Dei*—but only the sage can hear what, precisely, this Voice is saying.

"Fair Nottamun Town," by every indication, is a rendition of the stations of the spiritual Path—seven of them, in this version—in largely alchemical symbolism. The action takes place in an uncanny realm which is neither heaven, nor hell, nor this world, but a kind of Limbo. It is not, however, the Limbo of lost souls, but rather a "liminal" realm of spiritual potentials, similar in some ways to the Celtic otherworld, or the *alam al-mithal* of Sufism, the world where symbols appear as living beings—the intermediary or psychic plane. The initiation depicted relates primarily to the lesser or alchemical mysteries, whose field of action is precisely the psychic realm. If the greater or *pneumatic* mysteries pertain to the union of the human soul with God, the lesser mysteries, as we have seen above, have to do with the acquisition of a soul that can properly be called human. The path of this alchemy leads away from the subhuman periphery of the psyche and toward its human center, the primordial or Adamic state, where the soul is vertically intersected by the *axis mundi*, the ray of Spirit—a center which, in both Sufism and Eastern Orthodox Christian Hesychasm—is called the "Heart." It is from this point alone that the mystical ascent toward union with the Divine can begin: "None come to the Father," said Christ, the second Adam, "but through me." Nonetheless, the stations the mystical ascent are always prefigured, or reflected, on the psychic level, otherwise of the soul would have no access to Spirit, and the Way would be blocked. Therefore my exegesis will sometimes apply more to the psychic plane, sometimes more to the Spiritual.

"Nottamun" or "Nottingham" Town is the place of "naughting," the town where we travel to become "not." It thus corresponds with the Sufi *fana*, or self-annihilation. It is the town of the dead—not necessarily the physically dead, but those who are dead in this life—who, in the words of Muhammad (peace and blessings be upon him) have "died before they are made to die." As Omar Khayyam said, "Dawn is breaking and the caravan/Starts for the Dawn of Nothing—O make haste!" But it is also, on the negative side, the land of those who are dead to the Spirit, the living dead who make up sense-bound "normal" humanity, now seen as they really are from the vantage point of that other world: *hylic* (material) man as witnessed from a *psychic* and potentially *pneumatic* standpoint.

Each of the seven stations of the spiritual Path is rendered, in "Nottamun Town," as a polar opposition, whose synthesis opens the door to the next level. The seven are: High and Low; Masculine and Feminine; Young and Old; Inner and Outer; Wet and Dry; Hot and Cold; Life and Death. The synthesis of High and Low—Spirit and matter, or Source and manifestation—posits the psyche. The synthesis of the Masculine and Feminine poles of the psyche posits the inner world as opposed to the outer, the inner world where Youth and Age are one because time is transcended. The synthesis of Inner and Outer worlds posits the Heart, the vessel where Wet and Dry—feeling and thought—can unite. The synthesis of Wet and Dry posits the level of the Philosopher's Stone, where the will is tempered and submitted to God. The synthesis of Hot and Cold—of total intent and radical detachment—completes this tempering, and posits the final synthesis, that of Life and Death, where Reality is identified with neither this world nor the next, but with the eternal present which both includes them and transcends them.

In fair Nottamun Town, not a soul would look up, or down, to show the traveler the Way to where he already is, to Nottamun Town. And so Nottamun is neither heaven above nor hell below, but the psyche, the intermediary plane, the realm of all souls, including the psyche of the traveler, who is thus traveling through, and to, the place where he already is.

As Dante says in *Purgatorio* 11:91–92, "[To] return again/to where I am, I journey thus. . . ." The essence of the spiritual Path is to travel to where we already live, to become what we are. In Vedantic terms, *tat twam asi*: "That [Reality] you [already] are." "Not a soul, not a soul" is like a chant designed to remind us that the human soul, in the face of God, is nothing, just as the Arabic word for "nothing" is virtually the same as the Hebrew name for the first man: 'adam. That "the way to fair Nottamun Town" would be shown by looking up and looking down reveals Nottamun as the Jacob's Ladder, the *axis mundi* whose symbols include the sacred mountain, the Tree of Life and the human spinal column—the path which connects, but also separates, visible manifestation and invisible Source. That the souls in fact look straight ahead is ambiguous: the sense-bound living dead are blind to the *axis mundi*, the ray of Spirit which vertically intersects every point and every moment. On the other hand, the spiritual travelers, those who have died before they die, know to keep their hearts fixed on what Sufis call the *waqt*, the present spiritual moment, remembering God neither by looking up nor by looking down—neither, that is, out of the desire for Paradise nor the fear of Hell. And the forward-looking souls also represent the psychic plane, intermediate between the Spirit above and the material world below.

The establishment of the polarity between High and Low defines the *axis mundi* as itinerary, and the spiritual Path as vehicle. Zenith is the symbolic point toward which spiritual aspiration is directed and from which the Grace of God descends; among the three *gunas*—the three modes of *prakriti* or primal matter in Hindu philosophy—it is *sattwa*, purity and balance. Nadir symbolizes all that flees from God and resists His grace, but also that aspect of God which is hidden in and by His own manifestation, just as the *kundalini* or serpent-power, in *kundalini-yoga*, is hidden at the base of the spine. Among the *gunas* it is *tamas*, the mass of egoic impurity which separates us from God, but which is also, paradoxically, the potency or stored power which makes the spiritual journey possible. Ignited by God's grace, it is the fuel which feeds the fire of its own purification. And the synthesis of High and Low, of *sattwa* and *tamas*, is *rajas*, which in this case is the power of spiritual action, the ability to consciously travel the Path, the psyche in active mode, under the rule of the Spirit above, and able therefore to rule the passive materiality of *tamas* below.

This power is symbolized by the ambiguous mount of the traveler, which is a synthesis of opposites, simultaneously a horse (that is, a stallion), a mare, and an hermaphroditic mule. Its color is at once gray, red ("roany"), a combination of gray and green, and black. "Horse" represents the masculine power within the soul, "mare" the feminine power, and "mule" the balancing or neutralizing power: in alchemical terms, Sulfur, Quicksilver and Salt. This indicates that the spiritual Path requires both a masculine fighting energy and a feminine receptivity to grace, as well as an ability to transcend all polarities, including this one. The animal as a whole represents the entire psyche with its polarities and oppositions synthesized—full self-knowledge as vehicle for spiritual transformation.

And self-knowledge can never be complete until it includes the body too. The ten-toed steed the traveler rides is the human form, the psycho-physical vehicle that functions as the alchemical vessel, the *athanor*, in which Sulfur, Quicksilver, and Salt are cooked, till they turn into the Alchemical Gold. As human beings we are designed to become that which, in the sight of God, we already are—and the only way we can do this is by traveling on the spiritual Path. It does no good to stand still in what we *think* we've accomplished or solidify as who we *think* we really are. To stand still on the Path is to be thrown by the mount who is supposed to be carrying us forward, and end up torn, bruised and sitting in the dirt, in dead material conditions cut off from the Spirit, in what is below our full humanity. Our only recourse is to get right back on the horse that threw us and resume our journey, on the ten toes of our own two feet.

Green and gray symbolize youth and old age, spontaneity and wisdom, those aspects of God represented in the Bible by "behold, I make all things new" versus "I am Jehovah: I have not changed." Together they indicate, on the psycho-physical level, a synthesis of Innocence and Experience, of an ancient, saturnine wisdom with that youthful responsiveness to the quality of the moment which is wisdom's application. On another level, the gray mane and tail of the horse represent the outer world of material forms, subject to death and decay, and the "green stripe" on the horse's back the inner world of eternal life, where the green of moldering corpses is the doorway to the green fields of Paradise. (The same double symbolism of the color green, as life on the one hand and death's door to greater life on the other, appears in the green-skinned Osiris as judge of the dead.) The "green stripe" is also the *axis mundi* projected horizontally on the plane of time, resulting in a synthesis between goal-oriented spiritual aspiration and the sense of Divine Truth as already fully present in the eternal Now.

Red and black symbolize the tantric polarity between *Shakti*, dynamic potentiality, and *Shiva*, motionless act: the red of manifestation and activity vs. the black of the Formless Absolute. In the Taoist *T'ai Chi* (yin/yang sign), black (or dark blue) is the color of Yang and Heaven, red the color of Yin and Earth. [For a more detailed treatment of this tantric/alchemical polarity, see Titus

Burckhardt's *Alchemy: Science of the Cosmos, Science of the Soul.*]

Where the first polarity, between High and Low, is vertical, the second, Masculine and Feminine, is horizontal; so now the cross appears. As the polar union of High and Low invokes the polar union of Masculine and Feminine, or right and left—in which the polar union of Youth and Age is virtual, since sexual union is related to time and generation, while the transcendence of sexual polarity is also the transcendence of time, given that in the Kingdom of Heaven they "neither marry nor are given in marriage" [Mt. 22:30]—so the second and third unions invoke a fourth, that of Inner and Outer, the axis of which is "behind and before," thus describing the three-dimensional cross explained in such detail by René Guénon in *The Symbolism of the Cross.*

The King and Queen, a common symbol in alchemical iconography, represent Sulfur and Quicksilver, Spirit and soul—or, on the purely spiritual level, the union of *Shiva* and *Shakti,* the Divine Subject as absolute Witness and the Divine Object as universal manifestation in the mode of power. The union of Subject and Object posits the spiritual Center, another symbol of which is the Heart, which is the "center in the midst of conditions," just as the King and Queen are in the center of "a company more." Those "before" have the King and Queen behind them, out of their field of vision, as their unconscious motivating force, and are proceeding on foot; these are the *psychics* (referring not to people who read minds and tell fortunes, but to those whose understanding is limited to the psychological level)—the religious exoterics. Those "behind" the King and Queen have them in plain view, and are aristocratically mounted, symbolizing their transcendence of and control over their lower selves; these are the esoterics, the *gnostics* or *pneumatics.* And on another level, the King and the Queen are the Grace and Wisdom of God that simply carry us along, the hidden power that moves *behind* all the hard, trudging work of being good.

The dynamic polarity which empowers the spiritual journey now flows not between the poles of receptivity and action, but between esoteric and exoteric, that which is hidden and that which is revealed, both of which are shown as necessary to the process. The "stark nekkid drummer" represents the outer revelation of a hidden reality, since the purpose of the drum is to command attention, to proclaim something, while nakedness, in spiritual iconography (the Buddhist, for example), represents that which is beyond form. The drummer has "his hands in his bosom," that is, inside his shirt; but since he isn't wearing a shirt, the implication is that his hands are literally inside his chest, which identifies the beaten drum with the beating heart. (This identification of drum and heart is explicit, for example, in certain Native American tribes, where the two-beat line, "BOM-bom, BOM-bom," represents the heartbeat of the earth.)

The division between inner and outer establishes the *athenor*, the alchemical vessel, in which the transmutation of the soul takes place in secret, in a "hermetically sealed" space. To say that the King's and Queen's company "talked all the while, not a word did they say" indicates that the process is a mystery, something that takes place under seal of silence, like that of the mummers. It is not to be spoken of; and yet something within the traveler hears and is informed by the teaching emanating from the silence itself. Just as the profane mind literally can't stop talking but never really says anything, so the transmission of esoteric mysteries is given either in silence, or by indirect, allusive speech which is "foolishness to the wise" of this world.

In the *athenor*, the polar union of Wet and Dry can take place, this being, in alchemical terms, specifically the marriage of *dissolving* (as opposed to *coagulating*) Quicksilver and *fixing* (as opposed to *volatilizing*) Sulfur [cf. Burckhardt's *Alchemy*].[1]

On the psychic level, this is the union between feeling and thought; on the level of Spirit, it is the union between Love and Knowledge, between *bhaktic* energy and *jñanic* understanding, producing what one Christian saint called "sober inebriation," as in the line "I bought me a quart [of ale] to drive gladness away." Here both excessive spiritual intoxication (the rain) and excessive intellectual

---

1. Quicksilver and Sulfur, as symbols for the soul and the Spirit, each express themselves in two opposing forms. The soul alternately contracts and expands, freezes and melts; the Spirit enters this world to express Itself in form, then departs again from the world of form, and by so doing annihilates it.

dryness (the dust) are overcome, producing the state the Sufis call "drunk within and sober without": "They laughed and they smiled, not a soul did look gay."

To "set down on a hard, hot, cold-frozen stone" is to sit, like the Buddha, on the "adamantine spot," the diamond-hard point of spiritual stability, beyond all fluctuation. This is the penultimate station of the spiritual Path, here represented as the union of Hot and Cold—in alchemical terms, the marriage of *volatilizing* Sulfur and *coagulating* Quicksilver. As the marriage of Wet and Dry is the union of Love and Knowledge, so the marriage of Hot and Cold is the union of the human will with God's will, and of the human intellect with God's impassiveness. In the Zen phrase, "though my heart is on fire, my eyes are as cold as dead ashes." The restless psychic substance finally comes to rest on, and as, the Philosophers' Stone. Sitting on that Stone, the traveler is once again at "the center in the midst of conditions," the point of radical detachment from the relative world. Here that center of detachment is fully established, not merely vis-à-vis the "company" of the psyche, but in relation to the totality of manifest existence, the Buddhist "ten-thousand things": "Ten thousand stood around me, yet I 'uz alone." In Sufi terms, this is called "solitude in company," a solitude which is ultimately that of the transcendent Deity Himself. At one end of the spectrum, it represents the total detachment from this world of the realized contemplative; at the other, the truth that the God within us, the *atman*, the Divine Witness, sees and knows all phenomena as Himself.

From this fixed point, the final polarity, that of Life and Death, or existence and annihilation, is established and resolved. "Took my hat in my hands for to keep my head warm" sounds like another paradox, like the naked drummer with his hands inside his shirt or the ale which produces sobriety instead of drunkenness. But really it is more straightforward: the traveler is actually holding in his hands his own severed head. In Sufi symbolism, to be beheaded means that the power of the headstrong ego is broken, that one has passed into *fana*, or annihilation in God; in light of this, we may perhaps gain insight into those other headless yet still living figures in myth and folklore, like Washington Irving's "Headless Horseman," or the

Green Knight of the medieval romance "Sir Gawain and the Green Knight" by the Poet of the Pearl. In Sufism, *fana*, annihilation in God, is always paired with *baqa*, subsistence in God; to be beheaded and still live is to be annihilated in one's selfhood while subsisting in God as one of His Energies or Names.

More precisely, to hold one's severed head in one's hands is to witness the entirety of cerebral consciousness—the *ratio* of the scholastic philosophers—from the deeper standpoint of cardiac conscious, which the scholastics termed *Intellectus.* It is to realize the station of *jñana,* the direct knowledge of God by means of God's own self-knowledge, in which the psycho-physical self is now the object—"he"—and the subject is the Divine Self within us—"I." In the words of Meister Eckhart relating to this station, "My truest 'I' is God."

To say "Ten-thousand got drownded that never was born" is, in terms of the outer appearance of things, the Buddhist doctrine of *samsara*, the vision of all sentient beings coming into formal existence and leaving it again without attaining second birth, without once catching a glimpse of their own true nature. This is how the world must look to the enlightened sage, when viewed through the eye of compassion. On the level of inner meaning, however, it evokes the re-absorption of all manifest existence into its transcendent Principle. The annihilation-and-subsistence of the individual, the microcosm—*drowning* being a Sufi symbol of union with the Absolute—leads to the dissolution and restoration-in-God of the universe, the macrocosm. This is the vision of (in Frithjof Schuon's term) "*maya-in-divinis,*" which is both the knowledge that the Unity of God's Essence contains the seeds of the ten-thousand things, and the understanding that the things which make up manifest existence have never fundamentally departed from that Essence, that the entire pageant of universal manifestation, from the standpoint of Reality, never took place. In Buddhist terms, "*samsara* is *Nirvana*"; "all beings are enlightened from the beginning"; "from the beginning, not a thing is."

But what of the curse that's laid on the song, that whoever understands it will lose all his or her luck? Clearly this threat is there to divert the idle curiosity of those who have not received the inner call to approach God on the path of Knowledge, and to warn them of the very real and destructive consequences of prying into the esoteric mysteries on the basis of curiosity or worldly ambition. These others, however, to whom that call is more commanding than the fear of any earthly misfortune, will ultimately realize that the "luck" they have lost is nothing but the regime of fate, the chains of *karma*. To those in whom the Eye of the Heart is open, there is no longer any such thing as good fortune or misfortune on the plane of conditions, only the actions of God, which are manifestations in space and time of His attributes, and signs of His Presence.

4

HOLD ON!

AN ESSAY ON SPIRITUAL METHOD

EVERY FORM OF THE SPIRITUAL PATH requires both theory and practice, both a map of the route and a vehicle to carry us along it. The traditional Negro spiritual "Hold On!," in the version sung my Marian Anderson, is all about the particular spiritual method known as "invocatory prayer" or "prayer of the heart."

Most spirituals and traditional ballads in North America come to us through Evangelical Christians, and the reformed theology of Evangelical Christianity emphasizes that we are saved by God's grace received through faith, not by our own works. The doctrine of Sanctification suggests that a Christian who has been justified by Christ's death and resurrection may go beyond this initial Justification to reach spiritual perfection in this life, but the idea that such purgation could be the result of a formal spiritual method is generally foreign to Evangelical belief. And it is precisely this that makes it so strange to find in a traditional Negro spiritual a short but entirely accurate rendition of invocatory prayer, like that practiced in Eastern Orthodox Hesychasm or by the Sufis within Islam. What the Hindus call *japam*, the Sufis *dhikr* (remembrance), and the monks on Mt. Athos the Jesus Prayer or *mnimi Theou* (remembrance of God) undeniably appears in "Hold On"—but what knowledge could 19th-century Negro culture in the South have had of Athonite spirituality? Some of the lore in "Hold On" could have passed to slaves through Catholicism, especially in Louisiana, but the form of invocatory prayer that it presents remains more Eastern Orthodox than Catholic. When we encounter influences like this we must always begin by assuming their passage from one human being to another, not inspiration—nonetheless, direct inspiration by the Holy Spirit, received by deeply pious and serious Christians, cannot be entirely ruled out.

The spiritual Path can be defined as a path of purgation, a journey through Purgatory in this life. Anyone struggling to overcome the vices is on a purgatorial path, but the spiritual Path in the full sense of the term requires spiritual knowledge as well as spiritual struggle, or rather spiritual struggle in the light of spiritual knowledge. In traditional spirituals, this path of purgation is often symbolized by the hard labor of climbing a mountain. In the song "Great High Mountain" as sung by Dr. Ralph Stanley (I always want to call him *Rev.* Ralph Stanley, before I catch myself), the mountain of the spiritual Path is described as follows:

> Once I stood at the foot
> Of a great high mountain
> That I wanted so much to climb.
> And on top of this mountain
> Was a beautiful fountain
> That flows with the water of life.

Climbing a mountain is a universal symbol of spiritual advancement, a meaning readily suggested to Evangelical Christians by Mt. Sinai in the Old Testament and both the Mount of Transfiguration and Golgotha in the New, as well as the "great high mountain" of Rev. 21:10. But Ralph Stanley's "Great High Mountain" more specifically reproduces the Mount of Purgatory in Dante's *Purgatorio*, which Dante and Virgil climb by means of a spiral road leading upward from terrace to terrace, and at the summit of which lies the plateau of the Earthly Paradise that holds the fountain of the water of life, a fountain which divides into two streams: Lethe (the forgetfulness of pain and evil) and Eunoë (the "good mind," the knowledge of God). The fountain of the water of life appears in the Heavenly Jerusalem in the Book of Revelations, but our main Judeo-Christian image of the mountain with the fountain on top of it is from the *Divine Comedy*. So often in these pages I find myself returning to Dante, Christendom's premier poet, as if he were somehow the great, hidden theologian behind the folk metaphysics of the western world—an intuition which seems also to have been picked up by Loreena McKennit, the Celtic folksinger from Canada, in her song "Dante's Prayer."

But back to "Hold On." In Marian Anderson's version, the text goes like this:

> "Noah, Noah, let me come in
> The doors are fastened and the wind does spin"
> *Keep your hand on the plough,*
> *Hold on.*
>
> Noah said "You done lost your track
> Can't plough straight and keep a-lookin' back"
> *Keep your hand on the plough,*
> *Hold on.*
>
> Mary had a golden chain
> Every link was my Jesus' name
> *Keep your hand on the plough,*
> *Hold on.*
>
> Keep on ploughin' and don't you tire
> Every round goes higher and higher
> *Keep your hand on the plough,*
> *Hold on.*

The first stanza has to do with Noah's Ark as a symbol of *recollection*. In order perform any kind of prayer effectively—and this is even more true of invocatory prayer—one's psyche has to be sealed against the world. What really belongs to us, the various powers and faculties of the soul, have to be withdrawn from involvement with the outer world, and concentrated in the spiritual Heart. In the story of Noah's Ark from the Book of Genesis, these soul-powers are symbolized by the animals, who come in "two-by-two"—in both the masculine mode of spiritual warfare and the feminine mode of receptivity to God's grace. (This practice of recollection is probably also related to what the Jungian psychologists call "withdrawal of projections.") The Muslims have a legend that the Ark of Noah also carried the body of Adam, like ballast along the keel. The Ark *is* Adam, in one sense; the animals are his elementals. Adam could name all the animals in Eden because they were the outer projections of the Names of God that he, as representative of the human form—the center and epitome of God's cosmic manifestation—was composed of. And *recollection* is the withdrawal of these projections; once this recollection is complete, the ark of the spiritual Heart (the hidden or *arcane* center of the soul) has to be sealed and caulked against further intrusions. The voices crying to Noah to let them come in are the voices of worldly thoughts and concerns; they are voices out of the "storm of life." And while we may need to pay attention to *some* of these voices later on, for various practical purposes, when entering into the state of prayer they must be absolutely and ruthlessly excluded: let them die; let them drown; show them no mercy. In one sense, the spinning wind they are fleeing from is the wind of the Spirit (cf. Job, "Then the Lord spoke to Job out of the whirlwind," as well as the Qur'an, "There is no refuge from God but in Him.") Whatever in involved in worldly concerns will encounter the Spirit of God as a destructive flood or a punishing wind. But in another sense, this wind points to the activities of the Powers of the Air, all the elementals of the psyche that have become demonically swift, penetrating, distracting and chaotic because the soul has turned away from God. Whenever we make an intention to concentrate upon God unreservedly, all the parts of our soul that are still in rebellion against God will do whatever they can to distract us from such concentration; they will turn into a destructive whirlwind of thoughts, fears, glamours and passions. This is why the doors of the Ark must be fastened shut. As St. John of the Ladder says of *hesychia* (contemplative stillness):

> Close the door of your cell to your body, the door of your tongue to talk, and the gate within to evil spirits. The endurance of the sailor is tried by the noonday sun or when he is becalmed, and the endurance of the solitary is tested by his lack of necessary supplies. The one jumps into the water when he is impatient, the other goes in search of a crowd when he is discouraged.

The second stanza relates to what the Greek Fathers call the "incensive faculty." Whenever we are assailed by worldly thoughts, demonic suggestions or the voices of our own passions, these things must be vigorously repelled; we need to become "incensed" at them; this is the spiritual and most truly "righteous" use of anger. If we become angry at other people we are not concentrating upon God; what we really need is to become angry at our own anger. When Noah condemns the voices of the drowning people outside the Ark for having lost their track, he is actually repelling those thoughts that are not on the "straight path" toward God, the ones that keep "looking back" to the perishable, drowning outer world. And ultimately, this includes *all* thoughts; the presence of God is truly and deeply sensed only in the full silence of the mind. To look back is to let one's attention wander toward the world, and also toward one's self-image or ego—"the world" being nothing, in fact, but reality when seen "through a glass, darkly," in the ego's tarnished mirror. And one of the most subtle and insidious temptations to "look back," for those walking the spiritual Path, is the temptation to gauge one's own spiritual progress; this is why having a spiritual master or director is so useful. It is certainly up to us to examine our conscience, to bring all our vices and resistances to God into the full light of day so they can be dealt with. But for us to presume to determine for ourselves how far we have come on the spiritual Path is nothing but the Devil tempting us to turn away from God and toward the world of self-images. God may (or may not) unexpectedly reveal to us, for His own purposes, that we have indeed made spiritual progress, or perhaps that we have actually regressed. But as St. Silouan of Mt. Athos said, the two thoughts we must reject at all cost, the two most powerful of the Devil's temptations to spiritual travelers, are "I am a saint" and "I am damned"—what the Catholics call the sins of *presumption* and *despair*. Our responsibility on the spiritual Path is to put ourselves in God's hands, which entails giving up all interest in who we *think* we are, and accepting ourselves, unreservedly, as who God *knows* we are. Our knowledge of ourselves is partial and ephemeral; God's knowledge of us is our true being.

The first two stanzas, then, have to do with recollection, with the return to the fully human state, and thus with the Lesser or Psychic

Mysteries. They indicate the necessary preparation for invocatory prayer. The second two stanzas relate to the actual practice of such prayer, to spiritual ascent, and thus to the Greater or Spiritual Mysteries. "Mary had a golden chain/Every link was my Jesus' Name" clearly suggests the "prayer rope" of Eastern Orthodox Christianity, the prayer beads used by Hindus and Sufis, and the Catholic rosary, which are used in all these traditions as an aid to spiritual concentration. In the case of the rosary, one says either a "Hail Mary" or the Lord's Prayer while holding a particular bead between the fingers, but in the case of the Orthodox prayer-rope—which uses knots, not beads—one actually says (in certain forms, anyway) the Name of Jesus while grasping each knot: this, according to the Christian form, is the essence of invocatory prayer. (This "Jesus Prayer" may also take the form of "Lord have mercy"—*kyrie eleison* in Greek—or "Lord Jesus Christ have mercy on me, a sinner.") And though the name of Jesus appears in the Hail Mary, and the Lord's Prayer contains the words "hallowed be Thy Name," the line "every link was my Jesus' Name" suggests the Eastern Orthodox practice much more clearly than the Catholic one. The fact that the chain is "golden" indicates that invocatory prayer is the "royal road" of spiritual progress. And though the science of alchemy has to do with the Lesser Mysteries, not the Greater, the alchemical *silver* is symbolically related to the completion of these Lesser Mysteries, while the alchemical *gold* is like a reflection of the Greater or Spiritual mysteries on the lesser, psychic level.

But why is does the golden chain, every link of which is Jesus' name, belong to the Virgin Mary? Catholic tradition has it that St. Dominic received the rosary from Mary, who appeared to him in a vision. Historians have pointed out that forms of prayer similar to the rosary existed before St. Dominic's time, and the general embarrassment of contemporary Catholicism in the face of the supernatural has cast a shadow over the story of St. Dominic's vision of the Blessed Virgin. But there is nothing to prevent God from sending true visions to whomever He will, nor from renewing a past practice or blessing with His divine favor an already-existing one. In any case, the rosary has always been associated with Marian spirituality in the Catholic world, and still is to this day.

Furthermore, the origin of the complicated knot which characterizes the Eastern Orthodox prayer rope is also attributed to the Virgin [see "The Sword of the Spirit: The Making of an Orthodox Rosary" by D.M. Deed, in *The Sword of Gnosis*, ed. Jacob Needleman]. The Virgin Mary is associated with interior, invocatory prayer—the prayer of the Heart—because the essence of prayer is perfect receptivity to God's Grace and Power: "Let it be done unto me according to Thy Word (i.e., "Thy Name")." Just as Mary conceived the Christ through her receptivity to God's Word, and nurtured that Word in her womb, so the Christian who practices the Jesus Prayer nurtures Christ within his or her spiritual Heart, till He is fully formed in the soul, and the soul fully *con*formed to Him; this is the inner meaning of "My soul doth magnify the Lord."

The last stanza stresses the virtue of constancy in the practice of invocatory prayer, in line with St. Paul's direction to "pray without ceasing," which undoubtedly referred to the invocation of the Name of Jesus with every breath. As each "round" or cycle of the rosary or prayer-rope is completed, a higher level is reached on the spiral road that leads up the Mount of Purgatory, toward the fountain of the water of life—which, in Christian terms, is Christ Himself, who called Himself "a fountain of living water." This is why the prayer rope is sometimes called, in Old Slavonic, the *lestovka*, meaning "ladder."

But why is the practice of invocatory prayer, and prayer in general, compared to ploughing a field? In terms of pattern, ploughing is like the Prayer of the Heart in that it moves back and forth from one end of the field to the other in a continuous motion, like the rising and falling of the breath. And just as ploughing is what gets the field ready to receive the seed, so the Prayer of the Heart makes the soul capable of receiving the Word of God. Only God can send the Seed of His Word; there is no way we can do that for ourselves. But we can make ourselves ready to receive what God may be gracious enough to send. As one Sufi writer said, in regard to the spiritual symbolism that sometimes appears in dreams, "when the inspired soul [the soul that is beginning to open to Divine influence] is in the course of being transformed into the one at rest [the soul perfectly obedient to God's Will], flat plains appear, lying fallow for cultivation." And in the words of another, "Knowledge only saves us on condition that it enlists all that we are, only when it is a way and when it works and transforms and wounds our nature, even as the plough wounds the soil." Ploughing is difficult, rigorous; it entails suffering for both the ploughman and the earth. But though it seems destructive, its final end is purely creative. Ploughing a field breaks up the hardness of the soil so the seed can take root; ploughing the soul breaks up the "hardness of heart" that closes us to Divine Grace.

5

GREEN GROW THE RUSHES-O, *OR* THE DILLY SONG

A PYTHAGOREAN BALLAD FROM CORNWALL

THE NUMBER-SONG "Green Grow the Rushes-o" is said to be of Cornish origin; it was once used to teach Christians their catechism. The title of this song shows it to be about growth, and therefore about the creation or manifestation of the universe, and the various stages of it, from the One Creator in Genesis to the Twelve of completed manifestation, the Heavenly Jerusalem in the Book of Revelations.

It's not really possible to understand "Green Grow the Rushes-o" without getting some idea of what might be called "qualitative mathematics." We are used to thinking of numbers as purely quantitative; "three" or "four" can mean only three pigs or four chickens—three or four examples of a particular item. But there are also such things as "threeness" or "fourness," the particular *qualities* indicated by the numbers three and four. The idea of qualitative numbers, which was the basis of the mathematical theories of Pythagoras and Plato, can still be found in the English language. We speak of being "four-square for the right" (which is why 90 degree angles are called "right" angles), or of a "love-triangle," or of somebody being "two-faced."

The early Greek philosopher Pythagoras demonstrated how numbers can express themselves in terms of quality, not quantity;

he did so by defining the numerical ratios on which musical tones and scales are based. The Greeks, the Irish and many other ancient peoples had a whole science of musical modes or scales. The Greek modes—which come down to us, perhaps in altered form, through the church—included the Dorian, the Phrygian, the Lydian, the Mixolydian, the Hypodorian (or Aeolian), the Hypophrygian (or Ionian) and the Hypolydian. Each *mode* produces a different *mood* in the listener (the two words are related); some stimulate sleep, some healing, some grief, some battle-fury, some erotic desire. The song "Scarborough Fair," for example, uses an old balladic scale that matches the church version of the Dorian mode. And the folk and popular musicians of today still know something about the qualities of numbers as expressed through music: The key of D is considered right for Scottish aires (where nostalgia and battle-pride are the dominant emotions), the key of B-flat for the blues (where grief and eros predominate), etc.

"Green Grow the Rushes-o" is a tour through the various qualities of the numbers from One through Twelve. Each number represents a level of Being, from the original One who creates the world but does not become entangled with it—the "Unmoved Mover" of Aristotle—through the Twelve of the completed cycle, represented in the Christian tradition by the Heavenly Jerusalem, within which is the Tree of Life that produces twelve different fruits, each of which ripens in a different month (an obvious reference to the zodiac), and which (as in the song "O What a Beautiful City," sung by Ralph Stanley, Marian Anderson and many others) has

> Three gates in the north,
> Three gates in the south,
> Three gates in the east,
> And three gates in the west,
> Making it twelve gates into the city,
> Hallelujah.

According to mathematician Michael S. Schneider, in *A Beginner's Guide to Constructing the Universe*, dealing with the mathematics, geometry, metaphysics, cosmology, mythology and folklore of the numbers from One to Ten:

A personal inner significance was given to initiates who had achieved a degree of psychological purification and were ready for more serious growth and spiritual transformation. Since they were strictly confined to oral tradition, the details of what they were taught are not known. But it's no secret that many of the mystery schools of ancient cultures sought a spiritual rebirth within the individual using the zodiac as a teaching tool in an original twelve-step self-help program.

From myths, legends and art we know that the zodiac was used as a sublime allegory of initiation. The twelve cryptic zodiacal constellations were seen nightly by everyone; for the initiate, they were translated into tools of self-knowledge. The zodiac described the inner constitution of humans, the structure-function-order of ourselves, mirroring that of the universe. According to the ancients, the archetypal principles revealed by arithmetic and geometry, represented by the zodiac, seen manifest in the designs of nature, technology, art, the clock and calendar [twelve hours and twelve days], temple architecture, myths, measures [twelve inches to the foot], and whole societies have correspondence within each of us. The initiate was taught to see the world inside-out, to see the twelve-part wholes as our reflection. . . .

Although different myths were conceived for different cultures, each in its own way depicted the exploits of the unified Cosmic Being, the ideas of every age. The twelve attributes represented by the zodiac were assembled into an ideal teacher, who guided the spiritual welfare of humanity through that 2,160 year period [i.e., an age]. In their cryptic language, solar allegories described a plan of spiritual birth within ourselves, of purification through twelve types of ordeal.

The twelve signs of the zodiac, twelve disciples, twelve tribes and pantheon[s] of twelve gods and goddesses represent twelve archetypal principles within everyone. These are our own twelve phases of transformation, the soul's journey home with Odysseus through twelve ordeals, the stages of expanding growth necessary in order to become complete and enlightened. Each individual comprises all twelve aspects of the whole, and we will eventually find within ourselves the principles represented by the symbols.[1]

At this point I need to introduce a note of caution. When contemporary people encounter material like the above passage—or books like the one you are presently reading—they will either tend to dismiss it all as "mumbo-jumbo," or see it as a dangerous form of occultism, or say to themselves: "Cool! Now that we've got ahold of the mystical secrets, let's construct an esoteric religion for ourselves and begin the marketing process." But as for myself, I don't fall into any of these categories. When I encounter material like this, I see it as an illustration of the truth that "the heavens declare the glory of God," but I don't imagine that this kind of knowledge can be resurrected in a simple way and applied directly to our spiritual lives. In these latter days, a vast amount of archaic spiritual lore is being liberated from the tomb of ancient history, as part of "the resurrection of the dead." In its own context (or contexts) much of this lore is, or was, valid. It wasn't all just some kind of Satanism or black magic. But the one thing that can't be resurrected is that set of contexts themselves. In certain Hindu and Buddhist traditions, and maybe a few others, it may or may not still be possible to use the zodiac as a partial map for the spiritual Path. But in the Abrahamic religions (Judaism, Christianity and Islam), it can no longer work like this (except tangentially perhaps, in the rarest of instances), nor is this kind of cosmological esoterism really of central importance any more in *any* of the world religions. The quality of our times makes it of doubtful value, and fills it with many spiritual dangers. When ancient cosmological sciences are recovered, or partly recovered, in our times, without any unbroken teacher-student lineages surviving that could put them to wise and balanced use, and in a world where the dominant view is scientistic, not religious—where when we look up to the sky we immediately visualize black holes and quasars (or the Global Positioning System), not God and His angels—these ancient sciences tend to collect around forces that are opposed to traditional religion and "embarrassed" by the idea of God, if not

---

1. New York: Harper Collins Publishers Inc., 1994, pp 217–219.

consciously opposed to Him. And so the person who sees this material as a kind of dangerous occultism is actually half right. Here is a poem I wrote about this kind of danger, after a visit to Stonehenge in 2001—an ancient temple (older than the Druids) that is oriented to the path of the sun:

A Visit to the Stone Clock

Sun Moon and Stars work on wires, across an iron sky
Over bloody Stonehenge.

Wizards torture power
Out of known tensions of conjunction and opposition
To lay down on Britain
An iron rule.

They cry down the Guardians themselves, ground their
    massive charge—
Till ancient terror of magic sails along the lines
From stone to stone:
No mercy, only titanic power
In those sentinels.

May we never dare to remember
What they most certainly knew.

What I felt at Stonehenge, in other words, was magic, wizardry, not religious piety. The site may have begun as something higher, but in contemporary Britain it is part of the resurrection of the darker side of an ancient Paganism, plus various post-modern fantasies about what such Paganism might have been, which are rushing in to fill the gap left by the fall of British Christendom. Nonetheless, astronomical and zodiacal symbolisms appear in the Book of Revelations itself in relation to another temple, the Heavenly Jerusalem; and one of the most reliable ways of contemplating the beauty and majesty of God is still through witnessing the profound and fascinating order-within-order of God's creation, stretching from the subatomic level through all the rungs of the Jacob's ladder of matter and organic and human life, to the planets, the stars, and finally the totality of the visible universe. In the words of Maximos the Confessor:

> [The Logos, or Christ], while hiding Himself for our benefit in a mysterious way, in the logoi [the invisible designs or "words" of visible things], shows Himself to our minds to the extent of our ability to understand, through visible objects which act like letters of the alphabet, whole and complete both individually and when related together.

And according to St. Paul, in Romans 1:20:

> The invisible things of Him from the creation of the world are clearly seen, being understood by the things that are made, even His eternal power and Godhead.

In line with this kind of understanding, such books as *Nature's Destiny* by William Denton, *Darwin's Black Box* by Michael Behe and *Intelligent Design* by William Dembski represent a contemporary form of contemplation of the order of creation, a way of demonstrating, if not proving, that "the heavens declare the glory of God and the earth shows forth His handiwork." In view of this, we need to recognize that a contemplation of the universal order has always been a way to God, even if the specific forms this contemplation took in earlier ages are no longer viable, and sometimes even dangerous. When our ancestors investigated the laws of mathematics and geometry, the mysteries of the musical scale (like the Pythagoreans) or the regular polyhedra (like the Platonists), they were looking for the traces, the *vestigia*, of God in His creation— unlike most of our own scientists today, who are paid to seek technical mastery, not religious understanding. And to the degree that we ourselves are seeking God, we should salute those ancient religious scientists, and allow their doctrines to awaken in us a sense of the wonders of God's creation. This is not to say, of course, that the knowledge they came up with was never diverted in a magical direction. Magic was the ancient equivalent—partly at least—of our own technology, just as modern technology is clearly the equivalent of a great deal of Pagan magic, insofar as it seeks to use the secrets of nature for power and control. But if we know that the true control of events is in the hands of God, then we can listen to "the music of the spheres" according to those ancient scales without wrecking on the siren reefs of magic and occultism. The heavens do declare the glory of God; the earth does show forth His handiwork; from the standpoint of God's eternity, they are "a tree of life, that bare twelve manner of fruits, and yielded her fruit in every month: and the leaves of the tree were for the healing of the nations" [Rev. 22:2].

Here is the text of the song:

> I'll sing you one-o! Green grow the rushes-o!
> What is your one-o? One is one and all alone and evermore
>   shall it be so.
>
> I'll sing you two-o! Green grow the rushes-o!
> What is your two-o? Two, two the lily-white boys all clothed
>   in green-o!
> One is one and all alone and evermore shall it be so.
>
> I'll sing you three-o! Green grow the rushes-o!
> What is your three-o? Three, three, the rivals be.
> Two, two the lily-white boys.
> One is one and all alone and evermore shall it be so.
>
> I'll sing you four-o! Green grow the rushes-o!
> What is your four-o? Four, for the Gospel makers.
> Three, three, the rivals be.
> Two, two the lily-white boys.
> One is one and all alone and evermore shall it be so.
>
> I'll sing you five-o! Green grow the rushes-o!
> What is your five-o? Five for the symbols at your door.
> Four, for the Gospel makers.
> Three, three, the rivals be.
> Two, two the lily-white boys.
> One is one and all alone and evermore shall it be so.
>
> I'll sing you six-o! Green grow the rushes-o!
> What is your six-o? Six for the six proud walkers (night
>   walkers),
> Five for the symbols at your door.

Four, for the Gospel makers.
Three, three, the rivals be.
Two, two the lily-white boys.
One is one and all alone and evermore shall it be so.

I'll sing you seven-o! Green grow the rushes-o!
What is your seven-o? Seven for the stars in the sky.
Six for the six proud walkers.
Five for the symbols at your door.
Four, for the Gospel makers.
Three, three, the rivals be.
Two, two the lily-white boys.
One is one and all alone and evermore shall it be so.

I'll sing you eight-o! Green grow the rushes-o!
What is your eight-o? Eight for the April rainers (or bold
    rangers; or April raiders).
Seven for the stars in the sky.
Six for the six proud walkers.
Five for the symbols at your door.
Four, for the Gospel makers.
Three, three, the rivals be.
Two, two the lily-white boys.
One is one and all alone and evermore shall it be so.

I'll sing you nine-o! Green grow the rushes-o!
What is your nine-o? Nine for the nine bright shiners.
Eight for the April rainers.
Seven for the stars in the sky.
Six for the six proud walkers.
Five for the symbols at your door.
Four, for the Gospel makers.
Three, three, the rivals be.
Two, two the lily-white boys.
One is one and all alone and evermore shall it be so.

I'll sing you ten-o! Green grow the rushes-o!
What is your ten-o? Ten for the ten commandments.
Nine for the nine bright shiners.

Eight for the April rainers.
Seven for the stars in the sky.
Six for the six proud walkers.
Five for the symbols at your door.
Four, for the Gospel makers.
Three, three, the rivals be.
Two, two the lily-white boys.
One is one and all alone and evermore shall it be so.

I'll sing you eleven-o! Green grow the rushes-o!
What is your eleven-o? Eleven for the ones who went to
    heaven.
Ten for the ten commandments.
Nine for the nine bright shiners.
Eight for the April rainers.
Seven for the stars in the sky.
Six for the six proud walkers.
Five for the symbols at your door.
Four, for the Gospel makers.
Three, three, the rivals be.
Two, two the lily-white boys.
One is one and all alone and evermore shall it be so.

I'll sing you twelve-o! Green grow the rushes-o!
What is your twelve-o? Twelve for the twelve apostles.
Eleven for the ones who went to heaven.
Ten for the ten commandments.
Nine for the nine bright shiners.
Eight for the April rainers.
Seven for the stars in the sky.
Six for the six proud walkers.
Five for the symbols at your door.
Four, for the Gospel makers.
Three, three, the rivals be.
Two, two the lily-white boys.
One is one and all alone and evermore shall it be so.

The Oxford Book of English Traditional Verse gives the meanings of the verses as follows: One = God; Two = Christ and John the Baptist; Three = the Magi; Four = the Evangelists; Five = "possibly the Hebraic pentagon . . . but possibly also the five wounds of Christ"; Six = those who carried the water pots at the feast of Cana; Seven = the Great Bear or the planets; Eight = the Archangels; Nine = either the orders of Angels or the joys of Mary; Ten = Ten Commandments (self-explanatory); Eleven = the eleven apostles without Judas; Twelve = twelve Apostles (self-explanatory). Here we can see the rudimentary, *mnemonic* use of a song whose ultimate meanings go a lot deeper than just rote-learning your catechism. But since the doctrines of the Christian catechism are also a lot deeper than they appear on the surface, they are a valid and useful first attempt to explain "Green Grow the Rushes-o." Nor we should we sneer at simple mnemonic (memory-enhancing) devices. We all know the good use of "Thirty days have September, April, June, and November"; and the ability to store great masses of lore in memory (much of it, traditionally, in the form of song and poetry) is both integral to any traditional culture, and also good preliminary training for the deepest use of memory: the remembrance of God. A mind stocked with traditional spiritual lore (and all traditional lore is spiritual, to one degree or another) is well-weighted, ballasted like a good sailing ship needs to be, and therefore less inclined to turn with every wind than the "born yesterday" mind of the uncultivated, which is always ready to provide the knee-jerk reaction required of it by deceptive advertisers and dishonest politicians. Still, there is a lot more to "Green Grow the Rushes-o" than meets the ear or appears on the surface; so let's begin our dive to the depths of it, starting with the number One:

> I'll sing you one-o! Green grow the rushes-o!
> What is your one-o? One is one and all alone and evermore
>   shall it be so.

This is the universal orthodox doctrine of the One, the Absolute and Infinite. (The Hindus even go it one better; they reason that to call It "One" is already to imply all the other numbers, which is why they call it *advaita* instead, which means "not two.") If anything other than the Absolute existed, then the Absolute would not be

Absolute. On one occasion the Prophet Muhammad declared, "Before God created the universe He was alone, without a partner," to which his son-in-law Ali replied, "And He is even now as He was."

> I'll sing you two-o! Green grow the rushes-o!
> What is your two-o? Two, two the lily-white boys all clothed in   green-o!
> One is one and all alone and evermore shall it be so.

Two is the principle of manifestation. For anything to appear, it has to "stand out" against something else; the very word *exist* literally means "to stand out." (The same is true of our own ability to see or understand something, as when we say "I finally made him out on the hillside yonder" or "I couldn't make out what she was saying.") According to Plotinus, when God creates the elements of the universe, He first does it by contemplating them; He makes things *out*.

But who are these lily-white boys all dressed in green? Green is the color of growth, like the green rushes, and also of death—the color of moldering corpses. And white (the all-color), like black (the no-color), is the color of the Absolute when it *stands out* against the green of its own manifestation. (The One, in itself, is colorless, beyond even black and white.) Lily-white is the color of purity and virginity; it is pure of generation and in no way involved with it. The lily-white boys all dressed in green are there to remind us that within manifestation and becoming is a Something that is not involved in the dance of birth and death, which are merely Its outer garment. The inner ruling principle of all leafy green becoming is the whiteness of pure Being; if Being did not transcend becoming, nothing could ever become.

In relation to the color green, my wife, who grew up in Appalachian Kentucky, remembers this children's rhyme from her childhood:

> Green gravel, green gravel
> The grass is so green
> All over creation
> It's a sight to be seen

The rhyme went along with a dance where the children would

hold hands and turn in a circle, clockwise, while facing inward, then turn outward and begin to turn counter-clockwise. At the point of the turn they would recite:

> I wrote my love a letter
> And told him
> To *turn* his *head* a-*round*

In later years my wife talked to a folklorist at the University of Kentucky, who said that this game has been traced back as far as the 1870's, and that at one time the children used to put a mock grave in the center of the circle. This led her to speculate that the "green gravel" might actually refer to a mass of crumbled, moldy bones. Clockwise is the direction that the Buddhists and the Native Americans turn in their rituals; in terms of meteorology, it suggests the clockwise-tuning anti-cyclone that heralds fair weather in the northern hemisphere. Counter-clockwise, on the other hand, is the witch's direction, the direction of cyclones, twisters and dust-devils. To dance in a counter-clockwise direction is called "turning *widdershins*," which literally means "to be *contrary*." Muslims, however, also circumambulate the Kaaba counter-clockwise, as Eastern Orthodox Christians do their churches; in this case the symbolism has to do with the transcendence of form and the return to the Formless, a motion that is contrary to "the way of the world" (a meaning which, at one time, might have applied to the medieval Witches as well, or rather to the High Paganism of which they were a mere benighted remnant). To turn clockwise while facing inward towards a grave is to invoke God's blessings on the intent to die to oneself, which is sacred; to turn counterclockwise while facing outward, away from the grave, is to say, in effect, "when the sense of self-transcendence is forgotten, when the Center is lost, then all is dissipation and chaos, under the power of the Rulers of the Darkness of This World." But this darkness is compensated for by the last three verses:

> I wrote my love a letter
> And told him
> To *turn* his *head* a-*round*

"My love" is God, the Beloved. In these verses the children are invoking His attention and help to rescue them from the darkness of the outer world; if they are lost in the outer darkness, He must turn His attention to that darkness in order to save them, as when He is said to have "so loved the world that He sent His only-begotten Son, so that whoever believes in Him might not perish but have everlasting life." To turn one's head around is *metanoia*. It is our own repentance that invokes God's attention to us, just as it is God's eternal "turn" toward His created world which invokes that repentance in the first place. "Before you ask," God says, "I will answer."

In this rhyming dance, the color green symbolizes both life (the grass) and death (the gravel). And this is also the meaning of the green dress of the lily-white boys, which is there to remind us that, from God's point-of-view, life and death are one.

> I'll sing you three-o! Green grow the rushes-o!
> What is your three-o? Three, three, the rivals be.
> Two, two the lily-white boys.
> One is one and all alone and evermore shall it be so.

I imagine that *The Oxford Book of Traditional English Verse* and its sources picked "the Magi" as the meaning of the "rivals" because they didn't want to pick "the Trinity"—an attribution that is both metaphysically absurd, given the Unity of God, and also pretty disturbing to contemplate. But the Magi were no more rivals than the Persons of the Trinity are (though, as we shall see, the idea of "rivals" may have a very different meaning, in relation to these Persons, than what we usually think of as "rivalry.") The true rivals are the three elements of the human person: spirit, soul and body. "Flesh lusteth against Spirit and Spirit against flesh," said St. Paul; and both the Prophet Muhammad and many Eastern Orthodox Fathers, St. John of the Ladder for example, speak of the spiritual life as a "war against the soul." Soul must be conformed to Spirit during life by the breaking of self-will; if it is not, it will conform itself to the body instead, age as the body ages, and upon death become not one of the saints, but one of the *dead*. As it says in the old primitive Baptist funeral song "Am I Born to Die?," in Mason Brown and Chipper Thompson's version:

And am I born to die?
To lay this body down?
And must my trembling spirit fly
Into a world unknown?

Soon as from earth I go
What will become of me?
Eternal happiness, or Oh
Must then my portion be

A land of deepest shade
Unpierced by human thought
That dreary region of the dead
Where all things are forgot?

A similar rivalry often takes place in the world of human relations. We all know of the "love-triangle"; plenty of songs have been written about it, most of them (like "Mattie Groves") being tragedies. In the legends of King Arthur, the triangle between Arthur, Guinevere and Lancelot led to the destruction of the Round Table. The love between Guinevere and Arthur represented one true value (*agape*), and the love between Guinevere and Lancelot another (*eros*), but these values were totally incompatible on the plane of form. Without charity, love is barbarous; without *eros*, it has no depth. And only God can resolve an impossible contradiction like this; on its own plane, the triangle of attraction and repulsion, the vicious circle of love and hate, waltzing in 3/4 time, goes round and round forever. It is *made* impossible by God Himself (Who is a jealous God), precisely to teach us that man's extremity is God's opportunity, that with God, and God alone, all things are possible.

This kind of love-triangle is also reflected within the soul itself. In many medieval romances the beloved can only be won after overcoming dangerous trials, which often include slaying a monster or a dragon or an evil knight. It's as if an adulterous love-triangle exists between a Princess, a Dragon who keeps her captive, and a Hero who rescues her. (The Greek myth of Perseus and Andromeda and the sea monster Cetus is probably the earliest known version of this story.) In tales like this the Hero represents our will and rational intelligence in service to *conscience*, to the "still, small voice" of God within us, trying their best to follow what seems to be true and worthy, fighting against everything low and false, and sometimes going mad in the process. (Madness symbolizes the intuition of a Reality higher than conscious will and rational intelligence.) The Dragon is our passions, our unconscious ego, which holds our soul, the Princess, in bondage. And the Princess, rescued from the passions, is the spiritual Heart—our power to submit, in "unadulterated" purity, to the Will of God. Given that "two is company and three's a crowd," either the passions must kill the conscience, leaving the soul in bondage to the Devil, or the conscience must triumph over the passions, freeing the soul to be re-united with her True Love.

In terms of space and therefore of architecture, three is a number of stability. A four-sided rectangle or square can easily be deformed to produce a diamond-shaped figure or a lozenge, but this cannot be done to a triangle, as we can clearly see in the structure of a microwave tower, for example. But in terms of time, three is dynamic. A sine-wave, used to represent the wave-like nature of periodic motion, including frequencies and wavelengths of sound and light, has three "stations": a *peak*, a *trough*, and a *baseline*—the line that passes straight through the line of the wave itself, which alternately rises above and sinks below it. According to the philosopher Hegel in his concept of "dialectics," all motion is composed of a *thesis*, an original state of things; an *antithesis*, which arises from this thesis and contradicts it; and a *synthesis*, which resolves the contradiction between thesis and antithesis, and functions as a new *thesis* for the next dialectical round. According to his system, Hegel saw the unfolding of creation as a sort of *debate* as to the real nature of God, with its *pro* and *contra* positions, both of which must have some truth to them, but neither of which can have all the truth, since God is Transcendent and therefore incapable of being definitively described in terms other than Himself. The Sufi metaphysician Ibn al-'Arabi was undoubtedly referring to something similar when he said "there is war between the Names of God." As the traditional English ballad "Tom O'Bedlam's Song," expresses it,

I know more than Apollo [the Sun],

> For oft, when he lies sleeping
> I see the stars at mortal wars
>   In the wounded welkin weeping [*welkin* = "sky"]

In William Blake's poem *The Tyger* from *Songs of Experience*, the stanza

> When all the stars threw down their spears
> And watered Heaven with their tears
> Did He smile His work to see?
> Did He who made the Lamb make thee?

may thus refer to the despair of even the highest intellectual angels, the "*host* ('army') of heaven," before the impossible task of comprehending the terrible Majesty of God.

When Karl Marx reinterpreted Hegelian dialectics as being of better use in describing a human history based on class struggle than a metaphysical struggle of the "spirit" to understand itself, "Three, three the rivals be" took on a very grim and concrete meaning. But Hegel was right too; his idea of dialectics is actually quite accurate when it comes to the experience of trying to contemplate God, the Absolute One, as He is in Himself—a practice the Sufis call *fikr*. "God is this," we say to ourselves; "but no, wait a minute, God is *that*—hold on: God is also *both*, and neither." *Fikr* literally means "reflection". But according to the science of *nirukta* (see below, under Eleven), it can be poetically or analogically related to the word *faqr*, which means "poverty". A mirror must be empty of any images of its own for it to reflect truly; it is only through the recognition of our own poverty, our lack of any ability to comprehend or encompass God, that God can legitimately be contemplated; as Abu Bakr (the first Sunni Caliph) said, "To know that God cannot be known is to know God."

The Eastern Orthodox Christians have a similar doctrine in relation to the Holy Trinity, most fully worked out by St. John of Damascus; it is called *perichoresis*. (The Catholics call it *circumincession*.) This is the doctrine that each of the three Persons of the Trinity also contains and embraces the other two—which is why the English Christmas carol "I Saw Three Ships A-sailing," a song about the

Incarnation of Christ, has *three* ships: Christ is incarnate not simply as a distinct member of the Trinity, but carries with Him the fullness of the Godhead:

> I saw three ships a-sailing in
> On Christmas Day, on Christmas Day
> I saw three ships a-sailing in
> On Christmas Day in the morning

Perichoresis means "round-dance." It refers not only to the doctrine of the mutual inclusiveness of the Persons, but also to the dance of our consciousness when trying to contemplate God in terms of them. As St. Gregory Nazianzen said of it:

> I have hardly begun to think of the Unity before the Trinity bathes me in its splendor: I have hardly begun to think of the Trinity before the Unity seizes hold of me again. When one of the three presents itself to me I think it is the whole, so full to overflowing is my vision, so far beyond me does he reach. There is no room left in my mind, it is too limited to understand even one. When I combine the Three in one single thought, I see one great flame without being able to subdivide or analyse the single light.

Here we can see that the Persons of the Trinity are not rivals of *each other*, but rivals for *our attention*. It is this very "rivalry" which proves that God is totally beyond our discursive, *dialectical* understanding.

In terms of space, three is stability; it terms of time, it is dynamism. But in terms of eternity, which synthesizes time and space and also transcends them, three is the *perichoresis*, the motionless dynamism of the Trinity, which is neither fixed (fixity would make it comprehensible) nor passing (passage would make it imperfect). As St. Gregory Nazianzen says:

> The One enters into movement because of His fullness.
> The Two is transcended because the Godhead is beyond all opposition.
> Perfection is achieved in the Three who is the first to overcome the compositeness of the Two.

Thus the Godhead does not remain confined, nor does it spread out indefinitely.

It was the round-dance of *perichoresis* that T.S. Eliot was talking about in *The Four Quartets* by his phrase "the still point of the turning world."

As we have seen above in the exegesis of "Piri-miri-dictum Domini," the number three is traditionally the celestial or heavenly number, while the number four relates to the earth. The symbol for heaven is the circle (center, circumference, radius) and for earth, the square (the four directions). Everything above the point of four (three, two and one) is in the realm of the eternal God; everything below it, up to the number ten, has to do with the universe, with cosmic manifestation (though, as we shall see, the Transcendent God leaves His footprints here below as well).

The traditional symbols for "the Gospel makers," the Four Evangelists, are the Calf or Ox (St. Luke), the Lion (St. Mark), the Eagle (St. John) and the Man (St. Matthew), which are taken from the Four Living Creatures in Ezekiel 1:4–14, and are usually identified with the Four Beasts surrounding the Throne of the Lamb in St. John's vision recounted in Revelations. So Four could be called the number of what Frithjof Schuon terms "*maya-in-divinis*," the prefiguration of cosmic manifestation within the depths of the Divine Nature. In astrological terms, and given that over the last two thousand years the zodiacal signs have advanced by around 30 degrees from their earlier positions in relation to the points of the year, due to the precession of the equinoxes, the Ox relates to the sign of Taurus and the vernal equinox; the Lion, to Leo and the summer solstice; the Eagle to Scorpio and the autumnal equinox; and the Man to Aquarius and the winter solstice. And in terms of spiritual anthropology, the Ox is Plato's *appetitive faculty*, or desire; the Lion is the *incensive faculty* of Plato, will and aggression; the Man, the *rational faculty* (since the faculty proper to humanity, as opposed to all other natural and spiritual life forms, is the rational intellect); and the Eagle, the *Intellectual faculty* or *Nous*. (The Eagle soars in search of the spiritual Sun; his vision is sharp and far-reaching; and his *grasp* of his prey, like the Intellect's *apprehension* of a given Idea, is swift and unerring). The Lamb in Revelations is Jesus Christ, the "second Adam," the archetype of the human form in Eternity; the Four Beasts surrounding the Throne of the Lamb are His four primary faculties.

The four seasons, the four elements, the four directions have to do with the foundation and essential stability of cosmic manifestation. In the Masonic emblem, the compass relates to Heaven or the Three (the center of the circle it draws representing the Father, the circumference the Son, and the connecting radii the Holy Spirit), and the square to the solid, established, four-square Earth: when man is "edified," he becomes the *edifice* or temple wherein Heaven and Earth are united.

Four represents time enclosed within space. The round-dance of the Three, the *perichoresis*, exists beyond time; the cycle of the Four takes place squarely within this world. Its most complete expression, in terms of time, is the Hindu doctrine of the four *yugas* or world-ages which comprise an entire cycle of manifestation, a *mahayuga*. These are the *Satya-yuga* (in Greco-Roman terms, the Golden Age), the *Treta-yuga* (the Silver Age), the *Dvipara-yuga* (the Bronze Age) and the *Kali-yuga* (the Iron Age).

Turning again to the diagram of the sine-wave, we can see exactly how Three becomes Four. The sine-wave has three levels—peak, trough, and base-line—but four stations: peak (summer solstice); the point where the descending wave crosses the base-line (autumnal equinox); trough (winter solstice); and the point where the ascending wave crosses the base-line (vernal equinox). Once the four seasons and the four directions are established, as in the Native American medicine wheel, or any of the *mandalas* produced by other religions and cultures all over the world, then it is possible to do what the alchemists call "the rotation of the elements." By contemplating the distinct qualities of the four seasons over the course of the year— or, by the power of imagination, within a much shorter period—or by pondering the qualities of the four directions (sunrise, sunset, Pole Star etc.), we can detach and stand apart from the elements which compose the universe, and the corresponding elements which, in terms of the four souls we discovered in "Piri-miri-dictum Domini," make up the human form. If we have accomplished this we can reach the state the Eastern Orthodox theologians call *apatheia*, impassiveness. In Yeats' words, we can "Cast a cold eye / On life, on death." And once we have withdrawn all the projections we have made on the elemental world, once we have dis-identified with that world, then the elements which compose it are synthesized—after all, it was only our own egotistical identification with them that introduced strife into those elements in the first place, that divided them and set them at war.

> I'll sing you five-o! Green grow the rushes-o!
> What is your five-o? Five for the symbols at your door.
> Four, for the Gospel makers.
> Three, three, the rivals be.
> Two, two the lily-white boys.
> One is one and all alone and evermore shall it be so.

While pentacles have been used as metaphysical symbols and magical talismans by Hermeticists, Kabbalists, Masons, Witches and many others, with variously attributed meanings, the most universal and the most obvious meaning of the number five is "the human form." We have five senses, five limbs (including the head), and five fingers on each hand. And as we learned above under *four*, and in "Piri-miri-dictum Domini," the four souls, when viewed from the quintessential point in the midst of them, comprise the human form; when that form is seen in its fiveness, then it is fully objectified. Our knowledge of ourselves is partial and changing; God's knowledge of us is stable and complete. "The symbols at your door" seem to refer more directly to the five senses than anything else. The human body may be symbolized by a house, and if it is, the senses are the "door" between that house and the outer world. (William Blake symbolized them by windows instead: "Five windows light the caverned man.") The Sanskrit word for "man" is *manus*, which is related to the root for "mind" (as in the Latin *mens*). And the Latin word for "hand" is also *manus*. With our five human fingers we grasp physical objects; with our human mind we grasp ideas.

Michael Schneider shows how Five is the mathematical principle of the spiral, which expresses the principle of regeneration. The essence of the human form is self-transcendence; unlike the stars and the crystals, the animals and angels, we are created not as we are ultimately destined to be, but precisely in order to dominate ourselves, transcend ourselves, and so become ourselves. The road that leads from our inborn human potential to the final realization of that potential is the spiritual Path, and the form of that Path is spiral, like the way up the Mountain of Purgatory. As each round is of the spiral finished, as each spiritual life-task is completed, we reach a new station, a higher standpoint and a more comprehensive vision.

On the level of four, we appear as composed of elemental qualities, like the four humors of medieval medicine: yellow bile (choler), blood, phlegm, and black bile (melancholy). Fire predominates in the *choleric* temperament, whose characteristic emotions are sullenness and anger. Air rules the *sanguine* temperament, characterized by elation, flightiness and fear. Water determines the *phlegmatic* temperament, filled with sulkiness, feigned indifference, passive aggression and hurt feelings. And Earth predominates in the *melancholic* temperament, characterized by dryness, bitterness, depression. While we remain on the level of four, we are sunk in the undeveloped and unredeemed qualities of primal nature; we are elemental; elvish; not yet human. But as soon as the element Aether appears, called the *Quintessence*, the central fifth, then the human form is complete. The Aether, elemental reflection of the Formless Absolute, is (paradoxically, or seemingly so) the "field-aspect" of whatever is fully individuated. To the degree that we have entered into the matrix of the Quintessence, we are born as true individuals, with our own unique faces, our own personal names. No longer can we be entirely defined by our abstract, elemental qualities, by our zodiacal sign or our characteristic neuroses, our point on the enneagram or our Meyers-Briggs personality type. We have attained our incomparable essence; we have become our true selves. (The Hindu word for the Aether, the fifth element, is *akasha*, which, as the "akashic record," is considered to contain the recorded impressions not of generalized qualities, but of every particular form and event.)

At the level of Five, the human form takes its central place in the *mandala* of the four elements, the four seasons, the four directions—like Adam and Eve in the Garden of Eden, in the midst of the four rivers of Paradise. From this center, the four quarters of the *mandala* are revealed as reflections, in time, of the qualities of the Eternal Humanity, whose erect stature forms the axis around which they turn. In Eden, the human form is itself the Fountain of Living Waters, the Tree of Life.

> I'll sing you six-o! Green grow the rushes-o!
> What is your six-o? Six for the six proud walkers.
> Five for the symbols at your door.
> Four, for the Gospel makers.
> Three, three, the rivals be.
> Two, two the lily-white boys.
> One is one and all alone and evermore shall it be so.

The six proud walkers are the Six Days of Creation. In *A Beginner's Guide to Constructing the Universe*, Michael S. Schneider constructs Six as symbolizing, and incarnating, the concept of "Structure/Function/Order." Whatever has a special structure has an inherent function based on that structure; and every function, in terms of time, works itself out in a specific order or cycle. The six pots of water at the marriage feast of Cana [John 2:1–11] are related to the days of creation; their transmutation into wine by Jesus, in his first recorded miracle (which announces the scope and meaning of all that is to follow), symbolizes the transfiguration of the whole creation, the reversal of the cosmogonic process, the return of all things to their invisible Source in God. Six is Creation, and Apocatastasis. And the fact that his mother Mary asked him to perform this miracle reveals her as the passive point and matrix of the great turn or *metanoia* from creation to restoration, as Jesus is its active agent. What in the macrocosm is Apocatastasis, the restoration of all things, in the human microcosm is Remembrance, the prayer of the Heart. The walkers are "proud" by virtue of the exaltation felt by of all things, in the dawn of creation, at being freed from non-entity and brought out into actual existence, by what the Muslims call "the Breath of the Merciful," the Spirit of God that moved upon the face of waters [Genesis 1:2], on that day when "the morning stars sang together and all the sons of God shouted for joy" [Job 38:7]. And, after their absolute humiliation and *kenosis* (their radical emptying) at the point of the crucifixion, they are proud again—proud because Christ has triumphed over death, and they have triumphed with Him. As the poet John Donne put it, "O Death, thou shalt die!"

Six is the marriage of Heaven and Earth; the marriage of Heaven and Earth is the Temple; and the Temple is Mary. It was within her that the heavenly divinity and the earthly humanity of Jesus met and united. Under "three, three the rivals be," we saw how the Trinity is an eternal dynamism, a *perichoresis*; we also saw how the cosmic reflection of this *perichoresis* is the threefold *dialectic* of time. In Six, we have the union of these two aspects of Three, the union of time and Eternity.

Imagine the Trinity as a downward-pointing triangle hovering in the sky above a calm, waveless ocean; its reflection in the "lower waters" will be an upward-pointing triangle. What is eternal in the prototype is successive in the reflection, and there is a dynamic interchange between the simultaneity of the prototype and the sequentiality of the reflection. The closest physical analogy to this archetype of structure/function/order is what is called a "standing wave." Standing waves are produced by the repeated interference of two waves of identical frequency while moving in opposite directions through the same medium. If you have ever pounded (gently and rapidly) on a table holding a cup of liquid, like coffee, and seen how sometimes a pattern of motionless ridges will appear on the surface of it, you've seen a standing wave. The form of the wave is stationary, but the energy that maintains it is always in motion. In tantric terms, the moving energy of the wave is *shakti* (power, the feminine aspect) while the shape of the wave is *shaktiman* (power-holder, the masculine aspect). Given that modern physics has revealed matter and energy to be essentially equivalent, we can see how these two principles are related to (though certainly not identical with) the *forma* and *materia* of Aristotle. In the case of the statue of a lion made of gold, the gold is the matter, the *materia*, while the shape of the lion is the form, the *forma*. *Materia* is what allows *forma* to appear, to incarnate. Form is eternal and changeless, but whatever is material is ever-changing (like Madonna, the "material girl," who is always re-inventing herself). According to Aristotle, every real entity is the product of the union between *forma* and *materia*, between "heaven" and "earth."

Imagine again the downward-pointing triangle hovering over the calm, mirror-like ocean. Now forget the ocean, and bring the two together; when they unite, they form a six-pointed star, the famous Seal of Solomon, the symbol of the union between Heaven and Earth, and (by extension) of the Incarnation of Christ. Now separate the two triangles slightly, so that the point of the downward-pointing triangle rests on the base of the upward-pointing one, and the point of the upward-pointing triangle on the top line of the other. When drawn in this way, the Seal of Solomon demonstrates how the whole universe (the upward-pointing or *downward-widening* triangle) from the standpoint of Heaven, the celestial order, is only a single point of potential manifestation among an infinity of other points, and how the whole celestial order (the downward-pointed or *upward-widening* triangle) is nothing but a single point of potential realization from the standpoint of this material world.

Every temple is designed for the sole purpose of uniting Heaven and Earth. And according to the science of alchemy, the same is true of the temple of the human form. The purpose of the alchemical *magnum opus* is to "embody the Spirit and spiritualize the body," to unite Heaven and Earth within Man. Is it any wonder, then, that alchemy was highly developed in ancient China, given that Heaven, Earth and Man are the Grand Triad of primal principles underlying all traditional Chinese philosophy? In alchemical terms, Heaven is symbolized by Sulfur, Earth by Quicksilver, and Man by Salt; as Jesus said, "ye are the salt of the earth."

If Six appears as the six days of creation, in one sense it is the number of creation itself. When viewed in terms of space rather than time, it has to do with the six directions of space: the four points of the compass, plus zenith and nadir. And so Six is the power of God to pour His creative power into every direction of dimensional existence. In the Judeo-Christian tradition this power is symbolized by the six-winged seraphim, the highest angels, as they appear in Isaiah 6:1–3.

I'll sing you seven-o! Green grow the rushes-o!

What is your seven-o? Seven for the stars in the sky.
Six for the six proud walkers.
Five for the symbols at your door.
Four, for the Gospel makers.
Three, three, the rivals be.
Two, two the lily-white boys.
One is one and all alone and evermore shall it be so.

Six, as we have seen, is a number of dynamic interrelatedness and cosmic creativity, as expressed in the Seal of Solomon; it can be divided by 3, 2, 1 and itself; it is filled with internal structures, dynamics and relationships. And it is this very quality that can make it seem self-sufficient, as if creativity needed no Source beyond itself to draw upon, as if the cosmos could exist without the Transcendent God. The number assigned to the Antichrist in the Book of Revelations, 666, expresses this precise danger, which is another reason why the "six walkers" are called "proud." However, as soon as Six appears, Seven has already been posited. The six directions of space all radiate from a common Center; the six days of creation are followed by the Sabbath. In a way, those six days take place *within* the Sabbath, the "day of rest"; God does not create the world by effort and struggle because Infinite Power is necessarily effortless. When the Taoist adept practices *wu wei*, "doing without doing," he is putting himself in line with the Way, the *Tao*—with that divine effortlessness and impartiality which is the source of all power.

We have already said that Six is the Temple, and the Temple is the Mary. The aspect of the Virgin symbolized by Six is her motherhood; in herself, however, in the essence of her Eternal Virginity, her number is Seven. Seven is "virgin" not only because it is a prime number, divisible only by itself and One (in other words, impregnable only by God), but also because (unlike any other number between Two and Twelve, except Eleven) it cannot be perfectly constructed as a regular polygon (like a square or a triangle) using only a compass and a straightedge. Seven is the number of Virgin Space, three-dimensional in one sense, entirely beyond dimensions in another. She is the receptive matrix that allows all forms to appear exactly as they are, while in herself possessing no form but that very receptivity. The Virgin, in The Magnificat, can sing "my soul doth magnify the Lord" because she is His perfect mirror, completely without self-conceived image or externally inflicted stain; this is her "immaculate conception."

The "stars in the sky" could certainly be the Pleiades, the Seven Sisters; as a constellation composed (to most eyes) of seven stars, the Pleiades are like the signature of space appearing in space itself. But the "stars in the sky" are also, and more essentially, the *Septentrion*, the seven stars of the constellation Ursa Minor, the Little Bear (or Dipper), one of which is the Pole Star. In the 30th Canto of Dante's *Purgatorio*, the vision of Ursa Minor in the sky above the Earthly Paradise announces the coming of Beatrice in the Griffin Chariot, identified with the constellation of Ursa Major, two of whose stars, "the pointers," allow us to locate the Pole Star in the sky—which, according to the Franciscan monk St. Bernardine, is the origin of Mary's epithet "Star of the Sea." As the Pole Star is the fixed point that sailors steer by, so Mary is the unwavering guide of all souls through the deceitful, shifting currents and dangerous reefs of this world. And since throughout the *Divine Comedy* the Virgin is presented as the *archetype* of Beatrice, the one who sent her to guide Dante—which is why Beatrice can "point" to her—we can take the *Septentrion* as the symbol of the Virgin herself, with the Pole Star corresponding to the central point from which the six directions of space radiate. When we are perfectly receptive to God's will and grace like the Virgin is, we become "the still point of the turning world." (The *Septentrion*, or possibly Ursa Major, may be related to the seven lamps before the Throne of the Lamb [Rev. 4:5]—particularly in view of the fact that one of the epithets of the Virgin Mary is *Sedes Sapentiae*, "Throne of Wisdom.")

And the number Seven also has everything to do with music. There are seven musical keys (ignoring the sharps and flats); seven Greek modes; and the ladder of the octave from one *DO* to the next has seven steps. When we look at the Virgin in these terms, she suddenly appears as the vibratory power or *shakti* of the Father: His *wife*, His *weib*, His *wave*. In the Eastern Orthodox liturgy, the Jacob's ladder of Genesis 28:10–15 is seen as a "type" of the Virgin Mary. It is clear by this that the Virgin represents universal cosmic manifestation, the Great Chain of Being. The Latin word for "ladder" is *scalae*, from which we get our word for the musical "scale." According to Michael Schneider,[2]

> Western civilization's seven-note *diatonic* (from the Greek "across the tones") musical scale (the piano's white keys) has been used from time immemorial. In ancient times it was traditional to arrange the strings to play the scale downward, as if it were descending from heaven. The modern names of the seven familiar notes in descending order, DO-SI-LA-SOL-FA-MI-RE-DO, were proposed by Guido d'Arezzo, inventor of the musical staff, around AD 1000. These popular names are only the first letters of Latin words whose translation reveals a cosmological structure derived from an earlier age:

DOminus	"Lord"	Absolute
SIder	"Stars"	All Galaxies
LActea	"Milk"	Milky Way Galaxy
SOL	"Sun"	Sun
FAta	"Fate"	Planets
MIcrocosmos	"Small universe"	Earth
REgina Coeli	"Queen of the Heavens"	Moon
DOminus	"Lord"	Absolute

Universal manifestation or *Mahamaya* is a wave set vibrating between the poles of Transcendence and Immanence, between the twin truths that God is absolutely other than the universe, and that the universe, in its essential substance, though not as a collection of limited forms, is nothing other than God. When the sovereign hand of God touches the seven-stringed lyre of *Mahamaya*, which is the

---

2. *A Beginner's Guide to Constructing the Universe*, pp 234.

Great Chain or Scale of Being leading from this material world to the Eternal Throne of the Logos (appearing in the human microcosm as the seven *chakras* of the subtle nervous system), the forms of all things willingly come into existence; when He touches it again, they return in perfect obedience to the Virginal Silence that gave them birth. His first "composition" has more to do with Eve, who symbolizes the creative *Avidya-Maya* that veils God under the forms of His own manifestation; the Virgin, who is the "second Eve," is more directly related to the second set in His eternal performance, the one entitled *Vidya-Maya*, which reveals all things, in their metaphysical transparency, to be nothing other than words, and therefore signs, of their Creator.

> I'll sing you eight-o! Green grow the rushes-o!
> What is your eight-o? Eight for the April rainers.
> Seven for the stars in the sky.
> Six for the six proud walkers.
> Five for the symbols at your door.
> Four, for the Gospel makers.
> Three, three, the rivals be.
> Two, two the lily-white boys.
> One is one and all alone and evermore shall it be so.

If it weren't for Michael Schneider, this one would have stumped me. The text of the lines having to do with Eight has three variations in the version I've used: "April *rainers*," "April *raiders*," or "bold *rangers*." But since Schneider sees the number Eight as the principle of "periodic renewal," the true text must be "April rainers," the April showers that every year bring in the May flowers.

If Four is the four-square foundation of cosmic manifestation, the loom of cyclical time, and Twelve (as we shall see) the final form of the cycle-of-manifestation as "crystallized" in Eternity, Eight is the energy that moves through the cycle in a continuous and endless round. In Chinese philosophy, the cycle of Eight is represented by the eight trigrams, which when doubled form the 64 hexagrams of the *I Ching* or "Book of Changes." The world-conception of the Chinese, particularly in its Taoist rendition, is based on fluidity and change; stability is seen as achieved not by resisting change, but by responding to it, both receptively and creatively, both spontaneously and with due caution, deliberation and foresight. In accordance with this concept, the *Tao Te Ching* advises: "Move with the present."

In terms of the musical octave, seven notes of the diatonic scale return to their starting point at the eighth note; the cycle of Eight moves from *DO* to *DO*, which are essentially the same note. Nonetheless, the second *DO* is twice the frequency of the first (when ascending the scale) or one-half the frequency (when descending). And so the circle of the Eight is always describing a *helix* by moving up or down a vertical line passing through its center—which, when seen from a larger perspective, is itself not a perfectly straight line, but an arc of an even larger circle, and so on into ever larger (or ever smaller) orders of cycles-within-cycles. The return of the octave to a consonant but higher *DO* at the eighth note is taken by Eastern Orthodox Christians as a symbol of Christ's resurrection, the "Eighth Day of the week" that appears on no earthly calendar. And speaking in terms of space rather than time, the "Eight Clime" of the Muslims, a mysterious eighth continent that appears on no map, designates the subtle or intermediary plane, the location of the Earthly Paradise. Christ, in terms of the "glorified body" He assumed after His resurrection, is of one substance with that Paradise, which Dante places at the summit of the Mount of Purgatory, on the *eighth* level, beyond the seven terraces of purgation. If the circle symbolizes Heaven, and the square, the Earth, the octagon in Islam most often stands for the isthmus or *barzakh* between them— just as Dante's Earthly Paradise is the *barzakh* between the lower worlds and the Celestial Paradise itself. In order to represent this threefold hierarchy, mosques are often constructed with a circular dome resting on an octagonal drum, which itself rests on a square first storey.

According to the commentary on the *I Ching* known as the *Shuo Kua*, the eight trigrams are arranged, in the "Sequence of Later Heaven" or the "Inner-World Arrangement," as follows: *Ch'ien* (Heaven) at the winter solstice and northwest; *K'an* (Water) in the winter and north; *Ken* (Mountain) at the vernal equinox and northeast; *Chen* (Thunder) at spring and east; *Sun* (Wind; Wood) at the summer solstice and southeast; *Li* (Fire) at summer and south; *K'un* (Earth) at the vernal equinox and southwest; and *Tui* (Lake) at autumn and west. This cycle can be seen as a circular movement from Heaven (invisible Source or pure act) to Earth (receptive manifestation or pure potency) and back again; this motion is analogous to the "inbreathing and outbreathing of Brahman" in Hinduism, by which the entire universe, material, psychic and celestial, is periodically created (in the phase of outbreathing), then destroyed and reintegrated into its Source (in the phase of inbreathing), and then re-created, in an endless round. This cycle of breath, in terms not of the cosmic macrocosm but the human microcosm, is the basis of certain forms of Chinese yoga (as well as the *kriya-yoga* of the Hindus), whose goal is to produce a subtle or glorified body capable of inhabiting the Earthly Paradise, such as was attained by the "Eight Immortals." According to "The Book of Consciousness and Life," the *Hui Ming Ching*: "After [or 'according to'] the circulation in conformity with the law, there is a turn toward heaven when the breath is drawn in. When the breath flows out energy is directed towards the earth." (This motion is strictly analogous to the circulation of the creative wind from the Earthly Paradise to this world and back again in Canto XXVIII of Dante's *Purgatorio*.)

In Islamic tradition, the *nafas ar-Rahman* or "Breath of the Merciful" is the creative outbreathing by which Allah confers concrete existence on the *ayan al-thabita*, the "permanent archetypes," thus liberating them from the prison of non-entity. It is also the inbreathing (perhaps more accurately named *nafas ar-Rahim*, the "Breath of the Compassionate") by which He returns all things to Himself. In Islamic geometrical symbolism, the "outbreathing" of Allah is symbolized by an eight-pointed star composed of two intersecting squares, while His "inbreathing" is represented by the X-shaped figures that appear between such stars when they are set as closely together as possible, in parallel rows, like tiles on a wall or floor. And while Hinduism sees the outbreathing and inbreathing of Brahman as happening over vast cosmic cycles, the outbreathing and inbreathing of the Breath of the Merciful (at least according to one perspective, that of Asharite "occasionalism") can be considered to be complete in each separate instant.

I'll sing you nine-o! Green grow the rushes-o!
What is your nine-o? Nine for the nine bright shiners.
Eight for the April rainers.
Seven for the stars in the sky.
Six for the six proud walkers.
Five for the symbols at your door.
Four, for the Gospel makers.
Three, three, the rivals be.
Two, two the lily-white boys.
One is one and all alone and evermore shall it be so.

As we have seen, Six (as 2x3) is the dynamic polar union between the Transcendent Holy Trinity and its lower, threefold reflection in terms of cosmic becoming. Nine, as 3x3, is the Immanence of the Trinity throughout all creation; consequently it symbolizes the secret spiritual guidance and governance of the world, particularly as administered by the angelic orders. The Nine Bright Shiners are the Nine Choirs of Angels in the system of the church father Dionysius the Areopagite, which has been adopted by both the Eastern (Orthodox) and the Western (Catholic) churches.

The Nine Angelic Choirs are as follows (in descending order): the seraphim, the cherubim, the thrones, the dominions, the powers, the authorities, the principalities, the archangels, and the angels. Dionysius divides them into three ranks of three: The first rank (seraphim, cherubim, thrones) relate to God through knowledge and enlightenment; the second rank (dominions, powers [or, according to St. Bernard of Clairvaux, "principalities"], and authorities [Bernard's "powers"] relate to God through obedience; and the third rank (principalities [Bernard's "virtues"], archangels, angels) relate to Him through specific missions under the direction of the higher ranks. The first triad thus comprises the spirits of the Intellect, the second triad the spirits of the Will (not in self-determination but in perfect obedience), and the third triad the spirits of activity, who employ the higher powers of Intellect and Will to guide, protect and intervene in particular situations.

In St. Bernard's rendition of the Nine Choirs, the *angels* are those "each of whom is believed to be entrusted with the care of a particular person"—guardian angels, in other words; the *archangels* are those "who, knowing divine mysteries, are sent only on important or serious occasions"; the *virtues* are those "at whose bidding or by whose act signs and wonders appear in the elements or are formed in the elements, to instruct mortal men"; the *powers* are those "whose power checks the powers of darkness and binds the malignity of this air, so that it can do no evil, or any harm, unless it is for our good"—the spirits who come to the aid of exorcists; the *principalities* are those "by whose moderation and wisdom every power on earth is set up, kept within bounds, transferred, diminished, altered," the spirits who determine the economic and socio-political destinies of the world; the *dominions*, "ranked ... above all these orders, who are their ministering spirits"—the protecting, guiding and empowering "guardian angels of the angels" of the five lower choirs; the *thrones* are those who "are seated, and God is seated in them [in] most placid serenity, the peace which passes all understanding"—in other words, *the muses of contemplation*; the *cherubim* (whose apparitional forms in Ezekiel are like wheels whose rims are studded with eyes) "drink from the very fount of wisdom, which is the mouth of the Most High (Sirach [Ecclesiasticus] 24:5), and pour forth a stream of knowledge upon all the citizens of heaven; and finally the *seraphim* (who, in Ezekiel, appear with six wings) are "those who are aflame with the divine fire, and kindle the other citizens so that each is a burning and a shining light, burning with love, shining with knowledge (John 5:35)."

This quality of hidden spiritual governance appears in the mysterious design called the *enneagram*, which in our times has been used (or perhaps mis-used) mostly as a system of character-types. Helen Palmer got it from Claudio Naranjo, who got it from G.I. Gurdjieff, who got in from the Naqshbandiyya Order of Sufis, founded by Baha'uddin Naqshband, among whom it is known as the *naqsh*, the "design." According to Gurdjieff (whom we are free to believe or disbelieve) it originally came from Babylon. The enneagram is the diagram of any complete action, defined as any action which does not deviate from its original intent, but fulfills it perfectly, such that no "karmic residues" remain. It is drawn as a circle with nine equidistant points on its circumference. Within the circle an equilateral triangle is drawn, with its vertices numbered 9, 3, and 6. Also within the circle are inscribed a number of lines connecting points 1, 4, 2, 8, 5, 7 and 1, in that order. (This sequence of numbers is based on the decimal form of 1/7, which is a repeating decimal: 0.1428571428571428571... etc.) The *visible* action moves around the circumference of the circle from phase 1 to phase 9; the *unseen dynamics and correspondences* between the phases—the *angels* of them—move from 1 to 4 to 2 to 8 to 5 to 7 and back to 1.

The quality of Nine that relates it to the secret governance of the world also appears in the Greek myth of the Nine Muses, who *invisibly* inspire craftsmen pursuing the various arts. In Dante's *La Vita Nuova*, Nine is the number of Beatrice, his esoteric spiritual guide and the channel of Divine providence for him. The number Nine was also sacred to the Knights Templars. The rule of the Templars was composed by St. Bernard, who appears in the *Paradiso* to conduct Dante into the Empyrean where he beholds the Beatific Vision, leading one to speculate that the Templars may have considered themselves a kind of earthly expression of the Nine Angelic Choirs, with a role to play in the secret spiritual governance of the world.

Nine, like Three, is traditionally associated with the Great Goddess, the representative of God's providence immanent in conditions—who, when the Transcendent God is forgotten, becomes the regime of fearsome and mysterious Fate. This immanent providence is represented by the Egyptian ennead of nine gods, the *neteru*; by the nine Vestal Virgins sacred to the goddess Vesta; by the nine virgins in the college of St. Bridget; and by the *perichoresis* of the Holy Trinity, whereby each of the three Persons embraces the other two, resulting in a ninefold manifestation of God in the hidden dynamics of the universe.

> I'll sing you ten-o! Green grow the rushes-o!
> What is your ten-o? Ten for the ten commandments.
> Nine for the nine bright shiners.
> Eight for the April rainers.
> Seven for the stars in the sky.
> Six for the six proud walkers.
> Five for the symbols at your door.

Four, for the Gospel makers.
Three, three, the rivals be.
Two, two the lily-white boys.
One is one and all alone and evermore shall it be so.

Ten is the number of the fully-established system of manifestation under the rule of God. It is the "Kingdom" number, the number of "Thy will be done, on earth as it is in heaven." Ten is a development from Four, the foundation of cosmic manifestation. If Four is the foundation, Ten is the entire building, as we can see from the diagram known as the *tetractys*: a triangular arrangement of dots with four in the bottom row, three in the second row, two in the third row, and one at the top, all adding up to Ten. As a doubling of the Five of the human form, Ten has to do with the union of earthly humanity with our celestial archetype, through the medium of the Ten Commandments, the norms laid down by God for the conduct of our lives. These norms are not just the externally-imposed rules of some divine tyrant, but expressions of our intrinsic nature as God created us: to be commanded not to depart from our true nature is the furthest thing from tyranny; it is, precisely, freedom. (If there is anything we have truly forgotten in these latter days, it is that there is no freedom without limitation—that chaos, like alcoholism or drug addiction, is not freedom, but the worst tyranny imaginable.)

Moses, in Exodus, climbed Mt. Sinai to meet God, Who gave him the ten commandments upon which the society and spirituality of Israel were to be based. But when he came down again and found the children of Israel worshipping the Golden Calf, he broke these first tablets in fury. Then he went up Sinai for a second time, after which God gave him a different set of laws, laws cut down to the size of the Children of Israel in their present condition.

According to one interpretation of part of the *Zohar*—the classic of the Jewish Kabbalah—there are two Torahs: the Torah of the Tree of Life and the Torah of the Tree of the Knowledge of Good and Evil. The Torah of the Tree of Life is the Law as it was in Paradise before Adam sinned, the pure expression of God's creative power and wisdom, with no admixture of privation or evil. The Torah of the Tree of Knowledge is the Torah as we know it now in this fallen world. So the first tablets of the law that Moses destroyed appear to be the Torah of the Tree of Life. The ego of this fallen world cannot withstand, or understand, the Torah of the Tree of Life, where everything is lawful because everything is a manifestation or an act of God. It interprets the primal power and innocence of God's Self-manifestation not as a fullness of Divine Life into which no evil can come, but as a Divine validation of chaos, and thus a as license to harm oneself and others. What on a higher level of interpretation is Paradise (the summit of Sinai being the symbol of this higher level), on a lower one is a worship of the unredeemed passions, the Golden Calf. Moses brought the higher Law by which man is reunited to his Creator, but the Children of Israel could only see this as a re-validation of Paganism. (In the same way, St. Paul's doctrine that Christians were no longer under "the curse of the law" led to loose behavior in some instances, as in the excesses of the Christian *agape* feasts railed against in the epistle of Jude.) Therefore a second, edited version of the Torah, tailored to this fallen order of perception, had to be substituted, a Torah based on commands and prohibitions, on "the Knowledge of Good and Evil."

But behind the Tree of Knowledge, the Tree of Life still lives. The Torah of the Tree of Life is not simply a license to get away with anything because we are now "beyond good and evil." The Tree of Life *is* beyond good and evil—not because it is somehow half good and half evil, however, but because it is *all good*: whatever is good is necessarily real, and reality has no *real* opposite. The Torah of the Tree of Life, then, represents perfect obedience to the Torah of the Tree of Knowledge; as Jesus said, "I come not to destroy the law, but to fulfill it." But such perfect obedience cannot exist when our understanding of the Law remains on the rudimentary level of "do this but don't do that, because that's the rules," without really knowing why. In order for us to perfectly obey the law, our understanding of it must rise from the level of the will, which can choose to obey or disobey, and come to rest on the level of the Intellect, where all is Truth. Truth commands allegiance not through specific commands and prohibitions, but simply by being Itself. We follow It not through struggling to obey established rules of behavior—though this is a necessary first step, one which is never discarded, never "destroyed"—but simply by recognizing It for what It is.

The way back to the Torah of the Tree of Life lies through an inner understanding of the Ten Commandments. This inner understanding does not contradict the outer, behavioral one, but completes it. It shows how the practice of the virtues can be an "esoteric" practice in itself—a path to Wisdom.

Here are the Ten (in the Catholic rendition of them):

(1) *I am the Lord thy God . . . thou shalt have no other gods before me; thou shalt not make unto thee any graven image [of them]*. On the behavioral level, this is a prohibition of idolatry. To make images of, and worship, any of the cosmic powers—any of the numbers that follow the One—is forbidden. It is also forbidden to worship any image of the One, because an image of the One is no longer the One itself, but only a later, cosmic reflection of it. And what on the level of behavior is a prohibition, on the level of knowledge is simply the recognition that Absolute Reality *must* be One, that the idea of many gods, if we understand them as "multiple absolutes," is absurd.

(2) *Thou shalt not take the Name of the Lord thy God in vain.* This commandment forbids us both to pronounce the Name of God lightly or unthinkingly—as almost everybody does nowadays—as well as to take an oath in God's Name. That Name is eternal and unchanging, but our own ability, or willingness, to keep our promises is necessarily limited; therefore to swear in God's Name is like claiming for ourselves a Divine power we have no right to use or identify with. Just as Christ, the Word of the Father, is one with Him in "the unity of the Holy Spirit," so the *Shem ha-Mephorash*, the Holy and Unspeakable Name of God, is one with God Himself. This is why it was known to the High Priest alone, and was spoken by him only once a year, on the Day of Atonement, when he was alone with God in the Holy of Holies of the Temple at Jerusalem. The Name of God is the *presence* of God, and no one, not even the High Priest, has the power to command that presence. No man has either the right or the power to speak God's Name, except God Himself—which means that, when any human being speaks that Name, it is really God Who is speaking His Own Name within that person.

(3)   *Remember the Sabbath Day, to keep it holy.* On the outer level, this commandment prohibits us from engaging in profane pursuits on the Sabbath, and requires us to engage in divine worship. On the inner level, the Sabbath Day is the *present moment*: the only point where God's Eternity intersects with human time. To keep the Sabbath holy in this sense is to repel worldly thoughts, and consciously remember God, in this very moment. And as we have seen above, the most central and universal method for such remembrance of God is by means of His Name.

(4)   *Honor thy father and thy mother, that thy days may be long upon the land the Lord thy God has given thee.* On the outer level, this commandment demonstrates that no nation, no "social contract" can be stable and long-lasting without strong families, that no one who does not honor his parents can expect to receive honor from his children. In the words of Confucius,

> What is meant by saying, "To govern a state one must first bring order into one's family," is this: the man who, being incapable of educating his own family, is able to educate other men just doesn't exist. On which account the real man perfects his nation's culture without leaving his fireside.

Our parents are the "pillars of the temple" through which we came into this world, and as such they are the most intimate and natural symbols of the creative power of God. On the inner level, to honor one's father and mother is to recognize that all cosmic manifestation—*the land the Lord thy God has given thee*—is based on polarity, on the pairs-of-opposites. The union of father and mother is the union of God, as the creative Source of all things, with His *Shekhina* (His *Shakti*, His *Mahamaya*)—the principle of universal manifestation, Who is both the Mirror of His Names in the secrecy of His own nature, before the world was made [cf. Proverbs 8:22–26] and the Great Chain of Being which is His reflection in the created world of space, time, matter and energy [cf. Proverbs 8:27–31, and the first chapter of Genesis]. The "father" and "mother" we are to honor are the "spirit of God" and the "waters" upon whose face that spirit moved [Genesis 1:2]—the creative power of God whose work culminates in His creation of the Human Form in Genesis 1:27: "So God created man in His own image, in the image of God created He him; male and female created He them."

(5) *Thou shalt not kill.* On the outer level, this commandment prohibits the crime of murder; on the inner one, it forbids us to deny the reality of anything that actually *is real* because we fear it or are inimical to it. If we attempt to cut anything out of God's Reality by denying or ignoring it, we have essentially committed murder; to deny the reality of anything that in fact possesses reality is to deny the God Who created it.

(6) *Thou shalt not commit adultery.* Legally, this prohibits a married man or woman from having sexual relations with someone other than their spouse. Spiritually, it forbids us to *mix* our image of God with conceptions that are foreign to it, to create promiscuous, hybrid religions from elements taken from various traditions and contexts, which, by our own rebellious willfulness, we bring into an unholy union. If God is One, our conception of Him must remain undivided, and our spiritual practice kept firmly wedded to this Unity. In other words, the seventh commandment prohibits *syncretism.* If our conception of God becomes impure, fragmented, *adulterated*, we can no longer reach the Living God by means of it. Our consciousness is cut off from the spiritual level of things, where Unity reigns, and limited to the psychic level, where multiplicity imposes its deluded, polytheistic regime. Idols, like sexual objects, are always many—but God is our One and Only.

(7) *Thou shalt not steal.* In legal terms, this commandment forbids theft; in spiritual terms, it forbids appropriating to our ego something which that ego has no right to claim; in other words, it prohibits *identification*. In ourselves, apart from God, we are nothing—which is why the Hebrew name for the first man, *Adam* (which literally means "red clay") is almost identical, as we have seen above, to the Arabic word *'adam*, which means "nothing." We form our egos, our separate identities apart from God (or *apparently* apart from Him) by identifying with this or that experience, this or that object among the things, persons and situations of the outer world. These are the "stolen goods" that allow me to falsely claim autonomous and self-determined existence for myself, to imagine that I, like Lucifer, could separate myself from the will and

reality of God, and set myself up as ruler of a separate kingdom among the *shades*—the wraiths of the ego. To do so, however, is to build my house upon sand; it is to give my allegiance to a kingdom divided against itself, a kingdom that cannot stand.

(8)   *Thou shalt not bear false witness against thy neighbor.* In legal terms this commandment forbids giving false testimony in a court of law, and in a larger sense condemns all lying—because, given that everything we think or say or do is always done in the presence of a righteous Judge, we are always witnesses before His Court; consequently, every thought, word or act must always be true, "so help me God," or we will be found guilty of holding that Court in contempt. In the spiritual sense, to bear false witness against our neighbor is to see *anything* as other than it is. (To murder is to deny a thing's existence when it does in fact exist; to commit adultery is to associate a thing with something it has no essential relationship to, or place it in a context that is intrinsically foreign to it; to steal is to falsely see something other than oneself as pertaining to, or as being a part of, oneself; to bear false witness is to represent a thing—first to ourselves, and only later to others—as something it is not. Thus we can say that where commandments One through Four cover *sins of blasphemy* or *impiety*, commandments Five through Eight pertain to *sins of illusion*.)

The last two commandments, according to Catholic tradition, are: "Thou shalt not covet thy neighbor's wife" and "Thou shalt not covet thy neighbor's goods." However, the actual passage in which these appear, Genesis 20:17, runs as follows: "Thou shalt not covet thy neighbor's house, thou shalt not covet thy neighbor's wife, nor his manservant, nor his maidservant, nor his ox, nor his ass, nor any thing that is thy neighbor's." The Catholics split the Tenth commandment of Judaism into two: the prohibition against coveting one's neighbor's wife and his goods, respectively; the Jews split the First commandment in the above (Catholic) list into two, the first establishing the belief in God and the second prohibiting graven images; and the Protestants split the First commandment at a different place, between *I am the Lord thy God . . . thou shalt have no other gods before me* and *thou shalt not make unto thee any graven image.* But I have a particular reason for choosing the Catholic version:

because the Catholic Ten Commandments correspond more directly than the other two renditions with the Ten *Sefiroth* of the Kabbalistic Tree of Life, the hierarchy of Being or Divine Emanation that stretches from the Unknowable Essence of God, the *En Sof*, to this visible universe, or at least to its immediate prototype, the sefirah *Malkuth*, "Kingdom." How this can be explained historically (if it can) I leave to others to investigate; morphologically, however, it seems to be the case.

(9) *Thou shalt not covet thy neighbor's [house; thou shalt not covet thy neighbor's] wife.* Legally, this commandment prohibits us from coveting another man's wife, either by taking steps to possess her or by cultivating a murderous jealousy of her husband. (The Ninth commandment presumably refers to possession of one's neighbor's wife as a widow, since adultery is covered by the Seventh commandment, not the Ninth; this also clearly shows the connection between the Ninth command and the Fifth commandment, *thou shalt not kill*.) And on the inner level, this commandment forbids *spiritual jealousy.* Every individual has a unique spiritual destiny that is his or hers alone. A person may realize that destiny or betray it, but there is no way he or she can trade it for the destiny of another. The Hindu term for this unique destiny is *swadharma*, of which the Hindus say: "Better one's own duty, no matter how poorly performed, than the duty of another, no matter how well." Often we will think to ourselves: "If only I were like that other person—if only I actually *were* that other person. His or her spiritual path seems so much easier than mine; his or her spiritual destiny seems so much higher than mine. If only I were somebody else, my spiritual problems would be solved." Once this attitude is baldly stated, the foolishness and destructiveness of it become obvious. God requires of us the *one thing*, the one unique human soul, He made us responsible for. No one else can realize this spiritual potential for us, nor can we ever appropriate the spiritual potential of another. Our spiritual destiny, our *swadharma*, may seem to be so much lower or more difficult than somebody else's, but the fact remains that God requires of us *only this*—and if we fail to realize only this, then we will inherit eternal loss, while if we do realize it, then we have cut the one key that will open the single mansion in our Father's house

that has had our name on it from the foundation of the world. In the words of Mark 12:41–44:

> And Jesus sat over against the treasury, and beheld how the people cast money into the treasury: and many that were rich cast in much.
> And there came a certain poor widow, and she threw in two mites, which make a farthing.
> And he called unto him his disciples, and saith unto them, Verily I say unto you, That this poor widow hath cast more in, than all they which have cast into the treasury:
> For all they did cast in of their abundance; but she of her want did cast in all that she had, even all her living.

10)   *Thou shalt not covet thy neighbor's . . . manservant, nor his maidservant, nor his ox, nor his ass, nor any thing that is thy neighbor's.* To covet one's neighbor's wife is the sin of jealousy; to covet his goods is the sin of *envy*. The Tenth commandment prohibits us from angling to get ahold of another person's possessions by means other than burglary or armed robbery (which are covered by the Seventh commandment); in today's terms we might understand this prohibition as covering various legal, but nonetheless immoral, schemes and connivings. But on the spiritual level, these "possessions" represent the fruits of another person's spiritual labor. Just as we can never truly appropriate the spiritual destiny of another, so we can never really profit from the prayer and sacrifice and good works of another. If we want to travel the Path that leads to God, we will have to travel on our own two feet. Like the song says, "You've got to walk that lonesome valley / You've got to walk it by yourself / Nobody else can walk it for you / You've got to walk it by yourself." (Here we can see that, just as the first four commandments cover sins of impiety, and the next four, sins of illusion, the last two deal with sins that have particularly to do with misconceptions and false steps on the spiritual Path.)

Before we are finally finished with the number Ten, it remains only to show the correspondence between the Ten Commandments and the Ten *Sefiroth* of the kabbalistic Tree of Life, the powers or emanations of God whereby He creates "the heaven and the earth." I

believe it is very important to demonstrate this correspondence—
especially today. In these time we have seen the proliferation of
groups and individuals who want not only to split the Kabbalah off
from Judaism (which is to castrate it), but also to separate it from
any sense of the *moral requirements* for its practice. To people like
this (and they know who they are) the Kabbalah—or any esoteric
path, for that matter—is all about getting hold of the esoteric
secrets, and then using them to do *whatever they themselves decide.*
This is Satan's idea of esoterism—and Satan is nothing if not a good
marketing consultant. The idea that the Path might require something of *them*, that God might have laid down certain norms that
He expects us to follow whether we like it or not, is completely foreign to such people. That the path of the Kabbalah might require
one to be a practicing Jew, to follow certain rather strict moral rules,
and even to *obey a rabbi*—well, that takes all the fun out of it. (Like
comedian Don Novello, in the character of Father Guido Sarducci,
gossip columnist for *l'Osservatore Romano*, said about the cross as
the emblem of the Catholic Church: "The logo is a downer.") But if
such people (God willing) were to develop the kind of humility that
would demonstrate to them in no uncertain terms how it is impossible to possess *any* esoteric secrets in the truly *operative* sense without obedience to moral rules, they might come to the realization
that tedious, boring, bourgeois morality is actually *more esoteric*
than whatever their own favorite brand of Kabbalistic softwear, with
its glib and fascinating little secrets, graphically illustrated in living
color, could teach them in a million years.

The Ten *Sefiroth* are as follows: *Kether* ("Crown"; the unknowable
Divine Essence); *Hokhma* ("Wisdom"; the infinite radiance and
plenitude of Being); *Binah* ("[Discriminating] Intelligence," the
mirror-like, receptive void that reflects all things); *Chesed* ("Love");
Din or *Gevurah* ("Wrath [or Rigor]"); *Tifereth* ("Divine Beauty," the
ruling and balancing synthesis of all the *sefiroth*, the Heart of God);
Netsah ("Divine Victory," the life-giving masculine power of the
Creator); *Hod* ("Glory," the feminine, receptive, formative power of
the Creator); *Yesod* ("Foundation," the power that simultaneously
emanates manifest existence and reabsorbs it; the illusion that anything might exist apart from God; equivalent to the Hindu *Maha-*

maya); and finally *Malkhuth* ("Kingdom," the power that receives and consolidates all the possibilities latent in *Yesod*, and ultimately in all the *sefiroth*, and brings them into existence; the Immanence of God in His creation.)

1) *Kether* corresponds to *I am the Lord thy God . . . thou shalt have no other gods before me; thou shalt not make unto thee any graven image [of them]*. Given that the Divine Essence is unknowable, any image we might make of It or conception we might have of It is a lie, an illusion—and to worship illusions is to worship idols.

2) *Hokhma* corresponds to *Thou shalt not take the Name of the Lord God in vain*. Being is the symbol or Name of Beyond-being; the Name or Form of God emerges only from Beyond-being; to fail to realize this, to concretize God's Name by conceiving of it on a lower level, as if it were an independent reality in its own right, is to "take it in vain."

3) *Binah* corresponds to *Remember the Sabbath Day, to keep it holy*. The Sabbath is the eternal present; the present moment, void of past memories or future anticipations, is the mirror-like, receptive void that reflects all that the Name contains.

4) *Chesed*, Divine Love, corresponds to *Honor thy father and thy mother*; it is the love between the two primal principles, Chesed and Din, Love and Wrath, that generates all that is to follow, including you yourself. Only Chesed is properly Love; yet there is an intrinsic attraction between Love and Wrath. Love gives itself freely to all; Wrath ruthlessly wars against and destroys whatever would betray or menace Love.

5) *Din* or *Gevurah* corresponds to *Thou shalt not kill*: "Vengeance is mine, sayeth the Lord."

6) *Tifereth* corresponds to *Thou shalt not commit adultery*. The synthesis of all things as manifest in the celestial world is not promiscuity, but all-inclusiveness. If we place *Tifereth* on too low a level, however, if we approach it egotistically (which we will be tempted to do, since *Tifereth*, as the synthesis of all the emanated qualities or Names of God, is also the archetype of the human form, the Heart or Center of the Tree of Life), we will take it as a license for promiscuity, and so become *adulterers*. The human form is the synthesis of all things but it does not encompass all things; only God

does that. If we believe we can pursue every possible experience that exists as a latent potential within our human nature—that is, if we egotistically identify with God's all-inclusiveness—then we will ultimately lose the human form, and fall into the outer darkness.

7) *Netsah* corresponds to *Thou shalt not steal. Netsah* is the Generosity of God. Where all is given, nothing need be stolen; to steal in the presence of Absolute Generosity is precisely to refuse it.

8) *Hod* corresponds to *Thou shalt not bear false witness against thy neighbor*. By the power of *Hod*, all things in creation attain their true forms; to see or claim things to be other than they are is to pervert this power.

9) *Yesod* corresponds to *Thou shalt not covet thy neighbor's wife. Yesod* is the universal, subtle potential for concrete existence; she contains within her the eggs of all things before they come into this world. Only the qualities and life experiences she has in store for me, and me alone, really belong to me. To attempt to search out and appropriate potentials that are not destined for me is to refuse to be myself; it is to transform myself into an abortion, into something that no longer has either the right or the power to exist.

10) *Malkhuth*, "Kingdom," corresponds to *Thou shalt not covet . . . anything that is thy neighbor's. Malkhuth* is the *Avir*, the Aether. It is the "field-aspect" of whatever is most particular in manifest existence. On one level, *Malkhuth* is the receptive mirror of all that is above it, the wife of the King, of *Tifereth*. In this guise she is called the "lower woman." But in another sense, she represents all that is finally brought fully out into cosmic manifestation through human work—given that each man's work is his "calling," that we can only bring to completion, in the visible world, what God has already given us, in the invisible. (As we have seen above in the passage from Genesis 20:17, which is divided by the Catholics, though not by the Jews and the Protestants, into the last two commandments, the prohibition against coveting one's neighbor's wife could really be situated either before or after the prohibition against coveting his goods—and so a case could be made for inverting the order of the last two commandments, which would place coveting one's neighbor's goods under *Yesod*—the vessel where all the potentials for cosmic manifestation are collected—and coveting his wife

under *Malkhuth*, given that the Kingdom, as in so many mythologies the world over, is considered to be the spouse or "field-aspect" of the King.)

And lastly, what about the virtues? How does the work of *being good* relate to the act of *knowing truth*?

To avoid envy of other people's achievements is to concentrate on one's own work; the person who expects no support from others that he or she has not earned will become industrious—and the one capable of work to support himself will also be capable of constancy in spiritual practice; his spiritual life will be grounded in *Malkhuth*.

To avoid jealousy of another man's wife (or husband) is to learn what is intrinsically one's own, and gain the discrimination to separate it from what is not one's own. It teaches one to concentrate on the path that lies ahead and actually start to walk it, undistracted by fantasies and side-issues, in the realization that a distant but *real* goal is always better than a nearby but illusory one. The person who pays attention to his or her own duties and minds or his or her own business will be able to tap the specific spiritual potentials, out of *Yesod*, that he or she will really be able to actualize, and to ignore the ones that, as far as he or she is concerned, are barren.

To avoid lying is to gain the ability to see, and accept, things as they are—and whoever accepts things as they are will gain the power, out of *Hod*, to fully realize those subtle potentials that, in *Yesod*, were no more than insubstantial, though valid, intimations.

To avoid the temptation to steal—money, objects, ideas, attention—is to confront one's intrinsic poverty apart from God. And to confront one's intrinsic poverty is to open oneself to receive, from *Netsah*, the gifts of God that will make up all the provisions for one's journey.

To avoid the temptation to commit adultery is to overcome the more general temptation to believe that "the grass is always greener on the other side of the fence." It is to realize that "what is here is elsewhere; what is not here is nowhere." It is to be satisfied with one's lot, and therefore to find it beautiful. It is to learn—from *Tifereth*—"To see the world in a grain of sand / And heaven in a wild flower / To hold infinity in the palm of your hand / And eternity in an hour." Ultimately, it is to grasp, and embody, the true nature of the Human Form, through the realization that the Heart of that form contains all things. "Heaven and earth cannot contain Me," said God through Muhammad, "but the Heart of my willing slave can contain Me."

To overcome the temptation to murder and violence is to realize, in the face of *Din* or *Gevurah*, that God's Wrath is just, and also inescapable. If all punishments, in the rigor of God's justice, will inevitably be carried out, then we need not appoint ourselves as the agents of them, unless God commands us to do so. "Vengeance is Mine." And to be purified of anger is also to recognize that, in God's words through Muhammad, "My Mercy has precedence over My Wrath." It is to see *Gevurah* as the servant and emanation of *Chesed*, Divine Love; in the words of W. B. Yeats, "love is like the lion's tooth."

To be faithful in our religious duties, to go to church on Sunday, or the mosque on Friday, or the synagogue on Saturday; to remain constant in our own spiritual practices, in whatever it is we do to turn our hearts away from worldly distractions and remember God, is to open *Binah*, that pure and "sabbath" space where the grace of God can enter.

The most concentrated form of such practice is the invocation of the Name of God we have seen presented in songs like "Ma Journey": *dhikr*; *japam*; *mnimi Theou*. By this practice—having *become Binah*—we open ourselves to the influx of *Hokhma*, the radiance of Pure Being revealed (in us) as Divine Wisdom.

The final result of this practice—God willing—is to realize *Kether*, the One without a second, the Great Mystery—to both know and *be* the truth that "One is one and all alone and ever more shall it be so."

> I'll sing you eleven-o! Green grow the rushes-o!
> What is your eleven-o? Eleven for the ones who went to
>   heaven.
> Ten for the ten commandments.
> Nine for the nine bright shiners.
> Eight for the April rainers.
> Seven for the stars in the sky.
> Six for the six proud walkers.

Five for the symbols at your door
Four, for the Gospel makers.
Three, three, the rivals be.
Two, two the lily-white boys.
One is one and all alone and evermore shall it be so.

At the number Eleven, the great established system of Ten suddenly vanishes; absolute Transcendence unexpectedly reasserts Its rights over all manifest forms. Between one and twelve, Eleven is the only number other than Seven that cannot be constructed as a regular polygon using only a compass and a straight-edge—which, incidentally, is probably what makes Seven and Eleven the winning numbers in the game of dice, especially in view of the fact that many traditional games were originally designed to teach metaphysical principles ("jacks" for example). And while we can clearly visualize Seven as the six directions of space plus the Center, with Eleven we are out of luck. It cannot be simply constructed on a two-dimensional surface, nor can it be represented by a regular three-dimensional polyhedron (as Seven can by the octahedron). And as a prime number, it can be divided only by one and by itself. It is irreducible, aloof. As we have seen, Seven is the sign of pure, virginal space, the matrix that makes all geometrical forms possible, while not itself being one of them. But Eleven is not even the universal matrix; it is utterly transcendent. This is the inner meaning of the "eleven who went to heaven": since eleven is the number of pure Transcendence, those eleven "apostles" had to go up in smoke; they had to disappear from the field of manifestation entirely. According to the Hindu science of *nirukta*, words are related not by their etymological histories but by their inherent structures, regardless of how these structures may have developed over time; we might look at it as a kind of *philological crystallography*. Applying this science to the number eleven, we can immediately see, via what appears on the surface to be no more than a pun, how *eleven* relates to *elevation*. Just as eleven apostles were left, after Judas's suicide, to witness Jesus' ascension into heaven, so Eleven is the number that found no place in this world, the one that rose and flew away. In terms of Kabbalah, it would therefore represent the *En Sof*, the mysterious, unknowable, utterly transcendent Essence of God, beyond the ten *sefiroth* of the Tree of Life. (This Essence, in itself, is even beyond *Kether*, because *Kether* is the Essence as if it were *in relation* to the other *sefiroth*.) Eleven, as the number of Absolute Transcendence, is the passing away of the old heaven and the old earth [Rev. 21:1].

> I'll sing you twelve-o! Green grow the rushes-o!
> What is your twelve-o? Twelve for the twelve apostles.
> Eleven for the ones who went to heaven.
> Ten for the ten commandments.
> Nine for the nine bright shiners.
> Eight for the April rainers.
> Seven for the stars in the sky.
> Six for the six proud walkers.
> Five for the symbols at your door.
> Four, for the Gospel makers.
> Three, three, the rivals be.
> Two, two the lily-white boys.
> One is one and all alone and evermore shall it be so.

The ancient Greek philosopher Cleobulus proposed the following riddle: "A father has twelve children. Each has thirty daughters, black on one side and white on the other, and though they are immortal, they all die. Who is the father?" Answer: "The year." (The days of the year are mortal because they pass, and immortal because they always come again.) The number Twelve, on which "Green Grow the Rushes-O" is based, carries the quality of a complete, and therefore eternal, cycle of manifestation. Twelve is the number that reconciles the Sun (the year) and the Moon (the twelve months). The "inconstant" Moon represents time; the changeless Sun, eternity.

Twelve, like Six, is a temple number. Michael Schneider writes,

In ancient times design conveyed more than just style. Strict rules based on archetypal symbolism existed for the design of everything from kitchen utensils and furniture to temples and monuments. Temples and society were both meant to mediate and harmonize the heavens with the affairs of the people. Through number and geometric symbolism cosmology was built into the measures and proportions of sacred architecture. From prehistoric megaliths to Gothic cathedrals, temple design is imbedded with profound and surprising knowledge of relationships among the dimensions and cycles of the earth, moon, sun, planets, and stars. In accordance with the overall twelvefold structure, the temple was designed as a timekeeping device, a measuring tool, both a clock and a calendar mirroring the patterns of heaven on earth.[3]

Twelve is the number of the New Heaven and the New Earth [Rev. 21:1], and thus of the twelve-gated Heavenly Jerusalem: the summation and end of the cycle of manifestation. If Eleven is the end of time, Twelve is the dawning of Eternity. Twelve is the number of the *aion*: a complete cycle of time, seen—from the standpoint of Eternity—as a single "spacial" form. Societies that based their social and architectural structures on the number Twelve—like the Hebrews, the Etruscans, and other "twelve-tribe nations"—were attempting to see themselves *sub specie aeternitatis* ("under the category of eternity"); and the fact that Jesus Christ chose twelve apostles—not eleven, not thirteen—was right in line with His promise "Behold, I am with you always, even to the consummation of the *world*" (i.e., the "age"; the "*aion*"). According to Eastern Orthodox theologians, to see a cycle of time in its spacial simultaneity is to participate in what they call "aeonian time," a quality of time that is relatively "more eternal" than our linear, passing time, though still limited and temporal in relation to the Absolute Eternity of God.

The twelve gates of the Heavenly Jerusalem, with its twelve foundations, each of which is made of a different precious stone (precious stones symbolize *virtues crystallized as wisdoms*—in other words, *certainties*; cf. Prov. 8:11), and with the Tree of Life in the midst of it "that bare twelve manner of fruits, and yielded her fruit in every month" [Rev. 22:2], reveal it as a symbol of the new creation, next *aion*, and also as the final form of this one. The number Twelve has more internal structures, dynamics and relationships than any of the numbers before it, being divisible by 1, 2, 3, 4, 6 and itself—a quality that makes the science of astrology possible, with all its con-

3. *A Beginner's Guide to Constructing the Universe*, pp 211–212.

junctions, oppositions, squares, trines and sextiles. (Thirteen, on the other hand, is prime, divisible only by 1 and itself. Christ was the thirteenth among His twelve apostles; the Lamb is thirteenth in relation to the twelve gates, twelve fruits and twelve foundations of the New Jerusalem. As God's unique and "only begotten" Son, Christ is both the *center* of all relations and *beyond* all relations—as his agony in the Garden of Gethsemani demonstrated, when apostles fell asleep one-by-one, leaving Him to face His destiny alone. The number 13 is lucky because it symbolizes Christ, and unlucky because the worst blasphemy, and therefore the worst disaster, is to *mistake yourself for Christ*: "Can you drink the cup that I must drink?")

Nor is the Heavenly Jerusalem the only temple with twelve gates, and with the Tree of Life in the midst of it. In Chapter 7 of *Mirror of the Intellect*, Titus Burckhardt shows that the Paradise of Vaikuntha, heavenly home of the Hindu god Vishnu, also has twelve gates, and in the center of it grows the Tree of Life—a correspondence which demonstrates that celestial forms are not simply "beliefs" or "cultural artifacts"; they are sober realities of a higher order than this material world, every bit as objective—if not more so—as the rock in the field.

The Heavenly Jerusalem is described in Revelations 21:16 as being equal in height, length and breadth. It is therefore either an octahedron (two pyramids base-to-base) or a cube, like the Kaaba at Mecca (*kaaba* means "cube"). A cube has six faces, eight points and twelve edges; an octahedron has six points, eight faces and twelve edges. Thus the Heavenly Jerusalem reveals the Six of the union of the Trinity with its cosmic reflection, and the Eight of the periodic destruction and renewal of the universe, as embraced by the Twelve of eternity. If Six is the Temple considered as the union of Heaven and Earth, Twelve is the completed form of that Temple as emblem of the Divine Immanence: the entire cosmos revealed as God's Temple and His Throne. Thus the Heavenly Jerusalem is also the ultimate form of the Virgin Mary (*Sedes Sapentiae*), who is identified with the woman in Revelations 12:1, "clothed with the sun, and the moon under her feet, and upon her head a crown of twelve stars." For her to be clothed with the sun places her on the level of Spiritual reality, which is a higher order than the cycles of nature represented by the moon, which is now "under her feet." And the twelve stars show her to be the Heavenly Jerusalem in human form: In the eternal world, though not in this one, the Mother of the Lamb is also His Bride.

So "Green Grow the Rushes-O" is the "table of contents" of a complete traditional cosmology, from the One of the Sovereign Creator to the Twelve of His completed and eternal creation. But why does this song, like "The Twelve Days of Christmas" and many other counting-songs, repeat all the earlier verses within each later one? It does this to show that each later elaboration of cosmic manifestation contains all the earlier ones within it, which make up what might be called the "stem" of it, the Great Chain of Being that connects all manifest worlds back to their Transcendent Source—the Ground of Being—the One. Jean Ritchie's song "Tree in the Valley-o," which has a structure similar to a counting-song, is also about the Great Chain of Being—perhaps even incorporating some Kabbalistic influences, since the Chain is rendered in ten steps:

> There was a feather and a very fine feather and the finest feather you ever did see. . . .
> And the feather was on the wing and the wing was on the bird and the bird was in the egg and the egg was in the nest and the nest was on the twig and the twig was on the branch and the branch was on the limb and the limb was on the tree
> And the tree was away down in the valley-o.
> [*Tree in the Valley-O*, © 1952, 1965, Jean Ritchie, Geordie Music Publ. Co.]

The feather is the subtlest spiritual essence; the "valley-o" is this material world; the tree that connects the feather above (*Kether*?) to the valley below (*Malkhuth*?) is the Tree of Life.

To recognize the One within the many, as the Source of the many, is to realize the Immanence of God. And in terms of the spiritual Path, particularly in its Sufi rendition, all that really matters is: "One is one and all alone and ever more shall it be so." There is a Sufi story about a class of school children who were being taught how to write the letters of the alphabet by their teacher. Most of the pupils were progressing well, but there was one slow student who couldn't seem to get beyond the letter *Alif*—the first letter of the Arabic alphabet, corresponding to the English "A," which is also the sign used for the number one. (Our own numeral "1" is nearly identical to the Arabic *Alif*, on which it is based, except that the little "hook" is turned left instead of right.) The other children went on to other numbers, but the slow child felt that he had not yet fully mastered the *Alif*, so the teacher finally despaired of teaching him anything further and concentrated his efforts on the others.

Years later, after the children were grown, the aged teacher ran into a young man who introduced himself as the slow student he had taught so many years ago. "My old teacher!" he said, "how have you been? Since I last saw you I've been practicing my *Alif*; I think I've finally got the hang of it. Here, let me show you." The young man walked up at a wall and, using his finger like a pen, drew an *Alif* upon it—and the wall split in two.

One contains everything, but when we get involved in the numbers that come after it, our vision narrows down. The numbers from Two to Twelve (and, more particularly, from Four to Twelve) are the structures of cosmic existence; to each one of them corresponds a particular cosmological science. But cosmological sciences, like our own modern technology, tend to become over-developed—and if they go too far in their complexity and gigantism, they eventually hide the One. That's when the world of spiritual, psychic and subtle material knowledge becomes like Egypt when Moses came—filled with many deities, many powers, many secrets, but forgetful of the Living God. The Pharaoh's magicians knew much, but when the staff of Moses turned into a serpent, by the power of the One, it ate up all the serpents of magic. *Shema, Yisrael: Adonoi Elohenu, Adonoi Echad!* (Hear, O Israel: The Lord our God, the Lord is One!)

When our perception falls to the level of the numbers that come after One, it becomes *partial*; when we are at Two or Five or Nine, we can't see things as they really are because we are no longer completely *impartial*. The numbers from Two to Twelve are objects of knowledge, but the One is the Knower. The other numbers make up the forms of the universe, but the One is the Witness—not any of the objects seen by the eye, but the Seeing Eye itself. As it says in the Qur'an, *I will show them My signs on the horizons and in themselves, until they know that it is the truth. Is it not enough for you that I am Witness over all things?*

6

THREE BALLADS OF
FALL AND REDEMPTION

THOMAS RYMER, KEMP OWYNE,
& THE LAILY WORM AND
THE MACHREL OF THE SEA

A Word On, and To, the Neo-Pagans

IT'S NOT EASY TO SAY who the "Neo-Pagans" are. They are not a unified movement (though they are starting to get a bit "churchy"). But they certainly include the Nordic romantics of the "Goth" culture—the people who, when they think of Hyperborea, do not see the eternal spring of the Earthly Paradise, but sorcerers blasting people with magic wands and warriors cleaving skulls with battle-axes—as well as the softer Celtic romanticism which has produced River Dance and Celtic Woman and a lot of blurry, elvish elevator music. (Celtic Woman is the aesthetic solace offered by the elemental world to compensate for the loss of the human form—and that is a bad bargain.)

I maintain that some of the Neo-Pagans seem to have missed several important points, both about the spiritual life in general and about what Paganism originally was, in archaic times when it was spiritually alive and strong; and I know that as soon as I say this, some people will automatically see my misgivings as a kind of religious bigotry, as if I and my (supposed) political allies would immediately try to restore witch-burning if we ever came to power. This is not the case. Religious freedom, which I heartily support, necessarily includes freedom of speech in religious matters—which means that when I say that some of the Neo-Pagans seem to have missed certain points, I expect them to come forward and tell me the points they think *I* have missed. If we take refuge in "let us *not* reason together but simply grant everybody the right to his or her own opinion, in hopes that we will never encounter anything that contradicts it," then we have sealed ourselves off in separate bubbles; we have implicitly denied that religion refers to any objective Reality that we might conceivably reason together over. We have defined it as no more than this or that set of subjective fantasies or sentiments, and in so doing we have destroyed religion—*everybody's* religion.

Nowadays the term "esoteric," when applied to religion and spirituality, seems to automatically call up a spectrum of lurid, spooky images. Just as the word "supernatural" no longer suggests the realm of the Heavenly Father but rather the world of ghosts and demons and spirit entities, so the word "esoteric" calls up images not of a saint's cell, but a wizard's laboratory. In reality, esoterism is the same as straight orthodox religion, only more so. It is the ultimate flowering of the religious life, the life grounded in the virtues of faith in God, hope in God's Mercy, and love for God in His creation, and for that creation in God. If faith is "the presence of things hoped for, the evidence of things not seen," esoterism is divine Reality now seen not "through a glass, darkly," but rather "face to face." But many people—probably *most* people—who believe they are interested in things esoteric have little sense of the sacred, but are affected instead with a grim and/or pixyish fascination for psychic powers, magical talents, mysterious secrets and weird events. For such people—aided and abetted by the "permanent Halloween" now affecting this culture, the near universality of sinister and demonic images in the mass media—have little sense of the holy, but a definite, if not hyper-active, sense of the *uncanny*—so much so that to them (and to all of us, if we don't watch out), the uncanny will soon begin to seem normal, even prosaic.

And the Neo-Pagans are not the only ones attracted to the uncanny; plenty of scientists deal every day with uncannier realities than most Neo-Pagans have ever thought of. The fact is, our culture as a whole is losing the sense that a Supreme Being (insofar as we still believe in It) could be *good*. Either there is no Supreme Being, or whatever Supreme Being may be out there is not essentially good, but essentially *weird*. And given that Paganism is in many ways the coming thing, religiously speaking, our general cultural addiction to the uncanny is producing a collective sense that the inner meaning of Christianity, the esoteric part of it, is really Paganism in disguise. Christianity is "mere" morality, childish sentimentality, the opium of the people; it is the outer shell of an "esoteric" reality which, for those who can read the symbols, is really Paganism, or occultism, or magic. Church Christianity, as it is usually taught, is only for "laymen"; Paganism is the inner or *technical* aspect of the western spiritual tradition, the part reserved for the "priests"—that is, the magicians. And under the influence of this developing *zeitgeist*, the idea of a non-Christian Appalachia is also starting to make its appearance. There are no pious Christians out in those mountain cabins (except crazy, venal, drunken preachers), and never were; only Pagan witches and "wise-women" live there (which is not to say, of course, that no such people exist). The Foxfire folks, for all the good they have done in preserving native crafts and folkways, have also had a hand in spreading this "heathen" idea. (If you want a thorough expression of it, try to find a copy of *The Chymical Cook: A True Account of Mystical Initiation in the Georgia Woods* by Jay Bremyer.) But a non-Christian Appalachia is as much of a fantasy as a non-Christian Middle Ages—another re-writing of history that both high culture (the poet Ezra Pound, for example) and pop culture (the fantasy and science fiction folks) were working on for much of the last century. Remnants of folk magic certainly do exist in the Appalachians, in greatly diluted form—though it's hard to distinguish them now from the many newer *counterculture* forms of magic and occultism that started to come in during the 1960s—but the real spiritual and cultural backbone of the mountains is Christianity. The Cherokees, of course, *were* a non-Christian Appalachia, heirs of a high civilization and a deep spiritual tradition (carried on, in musical terms, by people like Walker Calhoun); but the white folks, the vast majority, for all their Indian blood, were and are Christians.

When the power of the Good descends, expressing itself through miracles of healing and spiritual regeneration, it happens through faith in Christ, not through soaking a potato in stump-water when the moon is full and burying it out back. The Neo-Pagans—at least those of them who practice Reiki and other methods of energy-healing, and know something about herbal medicine—have some definite things to contribute to the healing arts, I don't deny that. But if they claim (and some of them clearly do) that the real secret of Christianity is Paganism, I beg to differ with them on that point. In earlier world ages, before the Primordial Tradition was split when the Tower of Babel fell, the streams that became Judeo-Christianity and Hinduism, the Orphic-Pythagorean tradition of the Mediterranean and the Druid tradition of the Celtic peoples, were one river. But by the time Christianity was born, the Golden Age of Paganism, in both the classical world and Northern Europe, was long over.

I hasten to add that there is also an element in Neo-Paganism that is much more humanistic, or *human*, than the mere attraction to the uncanny—a spirit that is fairly well expressed, I would say, by the music of Van Morrison (which I love). The Neo-Pagans tend to be better read than most people (certainly more so than most New Age practitioners are), having inherited much of the literary culture that is being everywhere marginalized by the globally-dominant technical culture. May their wide reading, and the music they play, ultimately carry them across the track of the High King of Heaven, progressing with His retinue through the forest just ahead of them, beyond the next rise; some of their brothers and sisters ride with Him already.

I have taken this cultural and theological detour because I am about to present my exegesis of three traditional ballads that truly *are* uncanny, and do have a clear Pagan element—though behind them we can still discern the shadowy lineaments of the Primordial Tradition. These songs (and this is also true of "Lady Gay") clearly draw upon archaic, pre-Christian material, though Christianity was also undoubtedly an important influence as well. In "Thomas Rymer" the pre-Christian element, though dominant, is reconciled with the Christian world-view, and shown as in some ways complimentary to it. But in "Kemp Owyne" and "The Laily Worm and the

Machrel of the Sea," the archaic Pagan material is dominant. And
the story it tells, without any especial reference to the Christian
myth except in very peripheral terms, is that of a *fall* into the state of
nature, and the consequent loss of the human form. Many will
maintain that the uncanniness of these Pagan ballads only shows
the cultural marginalization of Paganism under Christian persecu-
tion; and there is undoubtedly some truth in this. But certain pre-
Christian religions—those of the Greeks and Romans in
particular—also possessed myths of the Fall, such as the loss of the
Paradise of Saturn, the defeat of the Titans, the metamorphoses
recounted by Ovid, the legend of Orpheus and Euridice, and the
story of the abduction of Helen in the *Iliad.* And to the degree that
these religions recognized the Fall but possessed no clear doctrine
of the Redemption—apart from a secret spiritual Way open only to
an initiatic elite—a sense of the uncanny, based on terror of magic
and despair in the face of an inexorable Fate, was inseparable from
them.

It is culturally and historically inaccurate to see Christianity *in
every case* as a foreign religion imposed by force of arms upon an
unwilling Pagan populace. The Pagan world of late antiquity often
had a vague sense of its own degeneracy, particularly after the Celtic
tribes had been conquered and assimilated by Rome; in some ways
it was waiting for Christ. If Druidism, for example, had still been
strong and healthy in the British Isles when Augustine came to
England, and Columba to Scotland, and Patrick to Ireland, the Isles
would never have converted, bloodlessly as they did, to Christianity.
According to some accounts, certain Druids were ready for Christianity, even expecting it (though of course many opposed it).
Because of the powers they still possessed, they knew that something of tremendous spiritual import had happened across sea, and
land, and sea again, far to the east, and were waiting for the waves of
it to finally crash against their white cliffs. They knew that Christ
had come. (A certain Aleut shaman had exactly the same relationship to St. Innocent of Alaska, who brought Eastern Orthodox
Christianity to the Aleutian Islands; he knew when the saint was
due to arrive, and gathered his people on shore to greet him.) The
major event in the transition from Paganism to Christianity was the

conversion of many of the Druids themselves; St. Columba is even recorded as saying "Christ is my Druid"—i.e., his *Geron*, his *Staretz*, his *Shaykh*, his *Pir* (in Greek, Russian, Arabic and Persian respectively)—his Spiritual Master.

"Thomas Rymer", "Kemp Owyne," and "The Laily Worm and the Machrel of the Sea" are more fragmentary, in mythological terms, than most of the other songs dealt with in this book; they are like great ruined cathedrals. And yet the outlines of an undoubtedly pre-Christian rendition of the Primordial Tradition—particularly that chapter of it which tells the story of the fall and redemption of both man and nature—can still be discerned within them. If today's Neo-Pagans clearly understood what these songs have to teach— that the world and the human soul *are* fallen, but that there is also a way of redemption from the conditions of this fallen world, a way out of the Regime of Nature, a way back to the Garden of Eden, then the name "Pagan" would no longer apply to them—at least in the sense in which it is used by Christian writers like C. S. Lewis and G. K. Chesterton, to denote a glamorized materialism that teaches that the human race is "OK" just as it is, that (as Freud maintained) the problem is not that we are ruled by our passions but only that we feel *guilty* for obeying them.

There certainly are many remnants of Paganism and folk magic in traditional English, Irish and Scottish ballads, as in the three Child ballads explicated in this chapter, and I wish the cultural historians, folklorists and mythographers all the luck in the world in their attempts to unearth and analyze these fragments. But I am on the trail not of the *remnants* of Paganism, but of what Paganism was when it was a living religious universe: not the bones of the ancestors, but something older, and deeper—and also newer: one more unique rendition of the *sophia perennis*, the perennial wisdom of the human race.

Thomas Rymer: The Redemption of Human Speech

When the clear vision of the heavenly worlds is lost, it is replaced by faith. And when faith is lost, or when it is successively placed upon lower and lower objects, then lesser worlds must stand hard duty for greater ones. Every world is a mask of God, but some worlds are a lot thicker and more opaque than others, a lot less amenable to demonstrating what Frithjof Schuon calls "the metaphysical transparency of phenomena." Nature as a theophany ("manifestation of God") is all grace, but Nature as a regime in herself is a hard taskmistress. Her teaching must contain an element of deception because, under present cosmic circumstances, no other tool is available to her.

The ballad of "Thomas Rymer" (which has been recorded in recent times by the traditional folk band Steeleye Span) shows how, when Heaven rises above us due to the darkening of our spiritual vision, until celestial realities become less and less plausible to us, the Regime of Nature takes over Heaven's work. Nature was always a face or mirror or symbol of Paradise, but when nature appears as an autonomous regime, a closed system, her ability to mirror "the deep things of God" is radically diminished.

The figure of Thomas Rymer, or Thomas the Rhymer (i.e., the Poet), is based on a historical figure, Thomas Learmonth of Erceldoune, who had a wide reputation as both a poet and a magician; his notoriety in this last regard nearly equalled that of Merlin himself. Like the Arabic poets in the days of the Prophet Muhammad, and like Pagan poets in all times and places, Thomas Rymer was inspired by those forces of the intermediary plane or psychic realm known to the Greeks as the Muses and to the Arabs as the *jinn*, a word related to the Latin *genii*. In modern times we might describe a certain poet as being a "genius"; in the old days, people would have said that he *had* a genius—a muse, in other words, or a familiar spirit. Poetry has always been related to magic, and this is precisely why, in a place and time where the reality of God has begun to fade in the minds of the people, the art of poetry is always in danger of becoming satanic.

The Queen of Elfland in this ballad is Thomas the Rhymer's muse, the embodiment of the superhuman glamour with which the Regime of Nature can sometimes clothe the lyric poet—before the credit card bill comes due, that is, as it did for Keats, and Shelley, and Dylan Thomas (and we can probably add names like Robert Johnson, Buddy Holly, Elvis Presley, Richard Fariña, Janis Joplin and Jimmi Hendrix to the list). Because there is a certain way receiving the blessing of that Regime which (as it were) turns those so blessed into heroes or demigods. All throughout the ancient world there were shrines dedicated to men and women who had become gods and goddesses after their death. And undoubtedly these great men and women were in some sense the "children" of, the emanations of, those deities, or archetypes, or Names of God which they had served during their lives. Of course it is true that no-one who has not encountered and willingly placed himself under the power of his or her archetype, or genius, or tutelary deity can lead a fully human life. But there is also a way in which one's relationship to his or her tutelary deity, especially if it is unconscious, can diminish that humanity. It is one thing to listen to the firm voice one's guardian angel, and quite another to be beguiled by the whispering of one's familiar spirit. And when we dream of being demigods because we are afraid to live as human beings, then, sometimes, the Regime of Nature will grant us that wish—a fate that poets and musicians and singers and other kinds of performers are always close to falling into. They are in danger of becoming "fey," a word meaning "fated," or "dedicated to a particular god" or "marked out for sacrifice to a particular deity," and which is also related to the word "fay," meaning "fairy." (Thus the character Morgan LeFay, from the legends of King Arthur, was both "Morrigan the Fairy" and "Morrigan the Fate.")

The one who was *fey* had one foot in the other world, and was considered doomed to die within a stated period. And one of the most common ways of becoming fey like this is through the worship of the aesthetic beauty and fascination of Nature as something separate from our full humanity—which is why this condition was traditionally, and often still is, a particular occupational hazard of poets. Those dedicated to the beauty and sublimity of nature as values in themselves, rather than as manifestations of nature's Divine Source, in light of our full humanity, attain "poetic immortality." In life, they are *fey*. In death, they become prisoners of the Queen of Faerie, dwellers in the "Land of the Ever-Young," hostages of the *Sidhe*.

Thankfully, this isn't Hell. Regretfully, this isn't Purgatory either. In Purgatory more is going on, there is more change, more development, more purifying suffering. The "Land of the Ever-Young" is, rather, the "Limbo" of Dante's *Inferno,* where all the classical poets live, surrounded by the beautiful forms of nature, but cut off from the light of the Holy Spirit. Nothing much changes there, millennium after millennium. In the Irish rendering of it, the poets and heroes feast on "swineflesh, milk and mead," and make love, forever, in endless glamour, subhuman and superhuman at the same time, to the beautiful women of Faerie, accompanied by the singing of exquisite poems, set to a music of unearthly loveliness, and heartrending nostalgia. But if anyone returns from that "all too divine" land to the world of earthly reality, if poet or hero ever sets foot, like the Irish hero Oisin did, on that all too human ground, he will shrivel up into a pitiful old man, and die in minutes. It had seemed to him as if only months had passed under that Faerie hill; in reality, centuries had passed. He had allowed himself to be beguiled by an inhuman beauty, only to learn that the sole way to the Transpersonal is through the Personal, that the only path beyond the human leads straight through the human—which is what Jesus meant when he said: "None come to the Father but through me." Aesthetic beauty is merely outside of time; love, however, even though it lives in the heart of time, is in Eternity already.

Merlin, like Thomas the Rhymer, had a deeper relationship to the Regime of Nature than that of the lyrical poet, though he undoubtedly entered the Realm of Faerie by essentially the same door. But he passed beyond the preliminary *aesthetic* pact with Elfland until he was able to conclude the greater *magical* or *technical* pact. By the power vested in him he created the fellowship of the Round Table, and that was a worthy creation. But to the degree that he used the Faerie Powers, he was also used by them; to the degree that he tapped the elemental forces of nature for his creative work, he fell under their power. The story of the final consequences of Merlin's covenant with the Queen of Elfland is a true instance of "poetic justice": In his old age he fell in love—idiotically, hopelessly, as old men sometimes do—with a young girl: Niniane (whose name, due to a scribal error, may originally have been Viviane, i.e. "Life"). She wrapped him around her little finger, till he had taught her all his magic; and because Merlin retained a part of his wisdom he knew exactly what was happening to him, but was powerless to prevent it. Finally Niniane, using one of Merlin's own spells, cast him into a magic sleep, or imprisoned him in a magic tower, or entangled him in a magic whitethorn hedge, from which no-one could ever free him—not even herself. He who was once a man was now nothing but a voice; locked in a powerful magic glamour, a superhuman trance with subhuman consequences, he awaits the Day of Judgment.

Thomas the Rhymer, however, was luckier than Merlin; he had a wiser and more merciful muse. Elfland, for him, was not simply that Limbo reserved for disobedient poets, that fallen paradise of aesthetic beauty and spiritual despair. Ultimately it was a spiritual Purgatory, though many of the stanzas that apparently recounted the purgatorial trials imposed on Thomas by the Queen of Elfland are regretfully lost. Outside the rigors of Thomas' journey through the other world, which are clearly purgatorial in their effect, all we have are these few tantalizing hints from Child's 37B, apparently set at the Queen of Elfland's court, which seem to show him resisting the temptation to break a magical taboo she has laid upon him (of the type the Irish call a *geis*) which requires him to speak to none but her:

> It's when she cam into the hall
>   I wat a weel bred man was he
> They've asked him question, one and all,
>   But he answered none but that fair ladie.
> O they speerd at her where she did him get,
>   And she told them at the Eildon tree
>
> . . . .

And though Thomas was abducted and indentured by the Queen for a period of seven years—which undoubtedly passed, in his own experience, as if they were seven days—the clear implication is that he was ultimately returned, a wiser man, to the human world, having earned by his trials the name of "True Thomas."

My "restoration" of a text of "Thomas Rymer" that makes mythopoetic sense is uncertain and conjectural. I have taken the text of Child 37C as the most complete, and have interpolated one stanza from Child 37B and four from his 37A. The stanza from 37B is only a slight variant, though it does carry some symbols worth commenting on, but the four from 37A could either represent an episode integral to a more complete version of the ballad, or a true alternative myth. That said, I will treat them as if they are integral to a more complete though unknown original, which had Thomas and the Queen of Elfland arriving at a "garden green" not once but twice. At their first entry Thomas is forbidden by the Queen to eat of the fruit of a tree that grows there, while at their second arrival, or their arrival at a second garden, she now invites him to eat of it, and he does so.

"Thomas Rymer" is about two things that are really one: the return of man to the Garden of Eden, and the spiritual redemption of a poet. They are revealed as one when we understand that when Adam ate of the Tree of the Knowledge of Good and Evil, this represented a fall from the integral knowledge seated in the Heart to the discursive knowledge lodged in the brain—in Scholastic terms, from *Intellectus* to *ratio*. *Intellectus* or *Nous* knows things in their unity; *ratio* sees things in terms of pairs of opposites, like good and evil—in other words, in terms of *comparisons* (ratios) between one thing and another; this is precisely what led Shakespeare to say "comparisons are odious." And the prime agent of this fall from *Intellectus* to *ratio* was the power human speech. Adam, in Eden, knew all things as words of God, because he was *obedient*; one phrase meaning "to obey" in Latin is *dicto audientem esse*, "to *listen* to (someone's) word or command." But after the serpent tempted Adam to see himself, not God, as the speaker, he fell out of God's perfect knowledge of him, and into the net of his own self-definition, which was the outer darkness. In other words, he stopped listening. And as soon as he began to define himself instead of submitting to God's true knowledge of him, he also began to define the world around him based on his own incomplete and fragmented self-image. He fell into the web of *maya*, a Sanskrit word that comes from a root meaning "to measure"; he mistook his verbal map of Reality for Reality itself. Whenever a poet begins to think of himself as a creator in his own right—as a *maker* rather than a *finder*—he blasphemously arrogates to himself the creative power of God, becomes entangled in the web of *maya*, and recapitulates the fall of man. (The idea of a poet as an independent creator or maker is a Renaissance conceit; the protagonist of Marlowe's play *Dr. Faustus* is a poet who invokes the power of demons so as to rival the Divine creativity. The Greek word *poietes* means "maker"; the Provençal word *troubadour*, on the other hand, comes from the verb *trobaire* meaning "to find or invent"—not "invent" in the sense of "contrive," but in the sense of letting something be blown into you like a *wind* [Latin *ventus*], something that comes to you by *inspiration*.) Plato, in his *Republic*, calls poets "liars." The Qur'an concurs in this opinion, maintaining that *most of them are liars*, and defining poets as people who *say that which they do not*.

My poetic mentor Lew Welch almost understood this. He said to me once: "Only poets know that words don't mean anything." He could have meant that, since words have no *intrinsic* meanings, they can mean anything we want them to; this is the nihilistic or even sacrilegious interpretation of the phrase that might actually have led him to commit suicide, seeing that the burden of trying to be in oneself the source of Truth is too great for any human being to bear. But inside that nihilistic shell is a sweet and edible nut: that only poets, intimate with language as they are, know that a whole unbroken world of Reality lives outside of, and completely untouched by, the words we try to catch it with—and that if we could stop naming things, we would see all things exactly as they are: and that would be the Garden of Paradise. Poets, at their best, are not caught in the net of language. Because they work with language like a carpenter does with boards or a mason with stones, they can see words (God willing) as objects outside themselves; they are no longer forced to live inside them. Words, to those poets who have triumphed over the great dangers of their calling, are not a mass of unconscious definitions of things like they are for most of us, but more like fish, or leaves, or birds. As Lew wrote in a poem entitled

"EVERYBODY CALLS ME TRICKY, BUT MY REAL NAME'S MR. EARL: A SERMON,"

> Those who live in the world of words kill us who seek
> Union with
> What goes on whether we look at it or not

—that is, with objective Reality. And the main resident in "the world of words"—the *only* resident, in fact—is the ego. It *does* try to kill us; it actually did kill Lew Welch. But Thomas the Rhymer was luckier. Under the rigorous tutelage of the Queen of Elfland he was relieved of his poetic arrogance and conceit; he stopped trying to be a *maker* and went back to being a *finder*. And given that the central distinguishing power of humanity is our God-given power of speech, the redemption of Thomas the Poet is also the redemption of Humanity itself. Here is the story of that redemption:

Thomas Rymer [Child 37C]

True Thomas lay on Huntlie bank,
   A ferlie [wonder] he spied wi' his ee,
And there he saw a lady bright,
   Come riding down by the Eildon Tree.

Her shirt was o the grass-green silk,
   Her mantle o the velvet fyne,
At ilka tett of her horse's mane
   Hang fifty siller bells and nine.

[alternate stanza, from 37B:]

The horse she rode on was dapple gray,
   And in her hand she held bells nine;
I thought I heard this fair lady say
   These fair siller bells they should a' be mine.

True Thomas, he pulld aff his cap,
   And louted low down to his knee:
"All hail, thou mighty Queen of Heaven!
   For thy peer on earth I never did see."

"O no, O no, Thomas,' she said,
  "That name does not belang to me;
I am but the queen of fair Elfland,
  That am hither come to visit thee.

"Harp and carp [play the harp and sing stories], Thomas,"
    she said,
  "Harp and carp along wi me,
And if ye dare to kiss my lips,
  Sure of your bodie I will be."

"Betide me weal, betide me woe,
  That weird shall never daunton me;"
Syne he has kissed her rosy lips,
  All underneath the Eildon Tree.

"Now, ye maun go wi me," she said,
  "True Thomas, ye maun go wi me,
And ye maun serve me seven years,
  Thro weal or woe, as may chance to be."

She mounted on her milk-white steed,
  She's taen True Thomas up behind,
And aye wheneer her bridle rung,
  The steed flew swifter than the wind.

O they rade on, and farther on,
  The steed gaed swifter than the wind,
Untill they reached a desart wide,
  And living land was left behind.

[from 37A]

O they rade on, and further on,
  Until they came to a garden green:
"Light down, light down, ye ladie free,
  Some of that fruit let me pull to thee."

"O no, O no, True Thomas," she says,
  "That fruit maun not be touched by thee,
For a' the plagues that are in hell
  Light on the fruit of this countrie.

"But I have a loaf here in my lap,
  Likewise a bottle of claret wine,
And now ere we go farther on,
  We'll rest a while, and ye may dine."

When he had eaten and drunk his fill,
  "Lay down your head upon my knee,"
The lady sayd, "ere we climb yon hill,
  And I will show you fairlies three.
[replacing similar stanza in 37C]

"O see ye not yon narrow road,
  So thick beset with thorns and briers?
That is the path of righteousness,
  Tho after it but few enquires.

"And see not ye that braid braid road,
  That lies across that lily leven?
That is the path of wickedness,
  Tho some call it the road to heaven.

"And see not ye that bonny road,
  That winds about the fernie brae?
That is the road to fair Elfland,
  Where thou and I this night maun gae.

"But, Thomas, ye maun hold your tongue,
  Whatever ye may hear or see,
For, if you speak word in Elflyn land,
  Ye'll neer get back to your ain countrie."

O they rade on, and farther on,
  And they waded thro rivers aboon the knee,
And they saw neither sun nor moon,
  But they heard the roaring of the sea.

It was mirk mirk night, and there was nae stern light,
  And they waded thro red blude to the knee;
For a' the blude that's shed on earth
  Rins thro the springs o that countrie.

Syne they came on to a garden green.
  And she pu'd an apple frae a tree:
"Take this for thy wages, True Thomas,
  It will give the tongue that can never lie."

"My tongue is mine ain," True Thomas said;
  "A gudely gift ye wad gie to me!
I neither dought to buy nor sell,
  At fair or tryst where I may be.

"I dought neither speak to prince or peer,
  Nor ask of grace from fair ladye:"
"Now hold thy peace," the lady said,
  "For as I say, so must it be."

He has gotten a coat of the even cloth,
  And a pair of shoes of velvet green,
And till seven years were gane and past
  True Thomas on earth was never seen.

That the Lady rides a dappled gray horse (in 37A) associates her with the Fates, the "gray ones"; the nine silver bells show her to be the Great Goddess, to whom the number Nine is sacred. The Goddess is most often associated with the Moon and her phases, and silver is the lunar metal. And the white horse of 37C identifies her as the Goddess in the guise of "Nightmare and her Ninefold," traditionally appearing as a white mare accompanied by nine foals; since Thomas is a poet, the Queen of Elfland and her nine bells obviously indicate the combined power of the Nine Muses, the source of poetic eloquence and verbal magic. According to Robert Graves, the Nightmare was charmed by the Norse god Odin, who bound her by her own hair (like the sea monster in the ballad of "Kemp Owyne" below)—an episode he identifies with these verses spoken in Shakespeare's *King Lear* by Edgar while feigning madness:

Swithold footed thrice the wold.
He met the Night-mare and her nine-fold,
Bid her alight and her troth plight,
And aroynt thee, witch, aroynt thee!

Thomas hails her as Queen of Heaven, an apparent mistake—yet
clearly she functions as a *reflection* of the Queen of Heaven, the Virgin Mary, in the underworld of the deep psyche. He kisses her
knowing that he is placing himself in her power; he is willing to risk
his freedom, and possibly his life, in his quest for poetic inspiration.

They ride "swifter than the wind" till they come to a "desert."
They are now in the Land of Death, where they encounter a "garden
green" which, with its tabooed fruit containing "a' the plagues that
are in hell," is obviously in some sense the Garden of Eden, but an
Eden more bewildering and uncanny than the first home of the
human race, in the time before the fall; it's more like a shadowy
underworld than a garden on the heights. Here the Queen offers
Thomas bread and wine and, unlike the "three babes" in "Lady
Gay," he eats and drinks. Under the influence of this mysterious
elfin Eucharist, he has a vision of the Three Roads of the Dead: the
road to Hell, the road to Heaven, and the road to Elfland. As a poet
dallying with the Queen of Elfland he is clearly not saved; and yet,
seeing that he is courageous, gallant, and faithful to his bargain with
her, neither is he damned. His destination is therefore Elfland, the
alam al-mithal, the world of poetic glamour, where the truths of the
Spiritual world appear in ambiguous, fascinating, mythopoetic
forms.

In order to enter Elfland they must wade through rivers, like the
four rivers of Paradise, two of which (the Hiddekel and Euphrates)
flow across the visible earth, and two (the Pison and Gihon) pass
through the invisible one [cf. Genesis 2:10–14]. And because Elfland
is the subtle aspect of the natural world that some have called "the
Etheric Plane," they hear the roaring of the sea, the primal chaos
underlying the visible, material world. Next they wade through a
river of blood, one that carries in its bed all the blood that's shed on
earth. This is the river of death, but of life too; the blood of that
river is all the hidden, stored-up vitality of terrestrial existence.

Now comes the *metanoia*, the great turn: Having apparently
remained faithful to the Queen's condition that he speak no word
for seven years while in Elfland, or speak only to her—a hard *geis* for
a poet—he is rewarded with fruit from one of the elvish trees. And if
the tree he encountered earlier in their journey is to be identified

with the Tree of the Knowledge of Good and Evil, the second tree can only be the Tree of Life, the virtue of whose fruit is that whoever eats of it can never again tell a lie; every word he or she speaks from that day forward will be the truth. And, of course, Thomas protests: how can he seduce women, turn a profit in business, or advance his interests at court if he can no longer lie? What he doesn't seem to realize is, that in order to *speak* the truth one must *know* the truth. Thomas is being given—against the will of his poetic ego—the gift of *omniscience*, like the runes that Odin gave his good right eye to possess; and all that Thomas the Rhymer is called upon to sacrifice is his precious *blarney*. Clearly he doesn't recognize a good deal even when it rides up and kisses him on the mouth. In indenturing himself to the Queen of Elfland he had hoped to gain the power of magical eloquence, the power *to make true whatever he chose to say.* He is given instead an infinitely greater power: the power *to say only what is true already.* Like all of us, but most especially like the poets, he believes that "my tongue is mine ane" [my own]. He is wrong. It is God alone who has the power, and the right, to determine what is true: what *He* says goes, because God is Truth. "So shall My word be that goeth forth out of My mouth: it shall not return unto me void, but it shall accomplish that which I please" [Isaiah 55:11]. If I speak *His* word, then I am a man; if I believe I can speak my own word to any true effect, with no regard to the *logoi*, the words of all things spoken by God from all eternity, then I am a liar and a fool.

And the spiritual method that produces this great *metanoia* is: to speak no word for profane purposes, to profane ears, but speak only to God. Whatever word I speak for the ears of This World is necessarily a lie; but if I speak only to God, and know it, and fulfill the conditions imposed by that deeply sacred and supremely fortunate dialogue—in other words, if I truly know that God is always listening—then I can speak the only truth; and that is the greatest good fortune imaginable. Truth is the fruit not of the Tree of the Knowledge of Good and Evil, but the Tree of Life.

Kemp Owyne *and* The Laily Worm
and the Machrel of the Sea:
The Fall Into, and Redemption
From, the Regime of Nature

These two ballads, which are similar enough to be considered variants of one original, express the disastrous consequences of the fall of humanity into the state of nature, of our identification with and worship of the material world. When this identification is so complete that neither we nor the society we live in feel any longer the dissonance between what we intrinsically are and what, through heedlessness and disobedience to our true nature, we have now become, the monstrous quality of our transformation is hidden from us. Here, however, it is revealed. In "Kemp Owyne," the child Dove Isabel is transformed into a half-human sea monster; in "The Laily Worm and the Machrel of the Sea," two children, a brother and sister, are changed into a worm and a fish. This is what the worship of the natural world apart from God ultimately results in—and if we will take a long, sober look at the quality of our popular culture and the images churned out by the mass media, we will realize not only that we do no longer fear this kind of transformation, but that in many ways we actively seek it.

Kemp Owyne

Her mother died when she was young,
   Which gave her cause to make great moan;
Her father married the warst woman
   That ever lived in Christendom.

She served her with foot and hand,
   In every thing that she could dee,
Till once, in an unlucky time,
   She threw her in ower Craigy's Sea.

Says, "Lie you there, dove Isabel,
   And all my sorrows lie with thee;

Till Kemp Owyne come ower the sea,
  And borrow [ransome] you with kisses three,
Let all the warld do what they will,
  Oh borrowed shall you never be!

Her breath grew strang, her hair grew lang,
  And twisted thrice about the tree,
And all the people, far and near,
  Thought that a savage beast was she.

These news did come to Kemp Owyne,
  Where he lived, far beyond the sea;
He hasted him to Craigy's Sea,
  And on the savage beast lookd he.

Her breath was strang, her hair was lang,
  And twisted was about the tree,
And with a swing she came about:
  "Come to Craigy's Sea, and kiss with me."

"Here is a royal belt," she cried,
  "That I have found in the green sea;
And while your body it is on,
  Drawn shall your blood never be;
But if you touch me, tail or fin,
  I vow my belt your death shall be."

He stepped in, gave her a kiss,
  The royal belt he brought him wi;
Her breath was strang, her hair was lang,
  And twisted twice about the tree,
And with a swing she came about:
  "Come to Craigy's Sea, and kiss with me."

"Here is a royal ring," she said,
  "That I have found in the green sea;
And while your finger it is on,
  Drawn shall your blood never be;
But if you touch me, tail or fin,
  I swear my ring your death shall be."

He stepped in, gave her a kiss,
　The royal ring he brought him wi;
Her breath was strang, her hair was lang,
　And twisted ance about the tree,
And with a swing she came about:
　"Come to Craigy's sea, and kiss with me.

"Here is a royal brand," she said,
　"That I have found in the green sea;
And while your body it is on,
　Drawn shall your blood never be;
But if you touch me, tail or fin,
　I swear my brand your death shall be."

He stepped in, gave her a kiss,
　The royal brand he brought him wi;
Her breath was sweet, her hair grew short,
　And twisted nane about the tree,
And smilingly she came about,
　As fair a woman as fair could be.

The dead mother in this ballad is the lost Paradise of Eden, which is both a realm in the subtle or psychic plane, and the natural world when recognized as a theophany, a manifestation of God. The father is, let us say, Adam: the human spiritual potential now diverted from its true object and married to "the warst woman that ever lived in Christendom": this fallen world. The mother is Eve as God created her; the "warst woman" is Eve after the fall. And the father's daughter, Dove Isabel, is the human soul. Dove Isabel does her best to protect herself by adapting to her fallen condition, by serving "the darkness of this world," but ultimately this is not possible for her: because this world is inexorable. And so ultimately she is thrown into "Craigy's Sea," and loses the human form. "Craigy," though it is a Scots proper name, also means "craggy"; so "Craigy's Sea" undoubtedly symbolizes unredeemed matter, the heartless instability and chaos underlying the apparent solidity of material existence. And the tree around which the monster's hair is wrapped is the Tree of the Knowledge of Good and Evil, which is the tree of manifest existence when cut off (apparently) from its Divine Source. That the monster's hair is wrapped around it three times indicates that the soul is triply fallen: it is fallen in its *will*, in its *affections*, and in its *thought*.

Kemp Owyne is a hero (*Kemp* means "champion"), which is apparently why he is able to restore Dove Isabel to human form; but how he comes by this power is not apparent. Clearly he must incarnate a spiritual quality higher than the state of fallen nature, but since the form and source of this power are not explained, his advent constitutes a kind of *deus ex machina*. Like Sir Gawain in the Arthurian romance *The Loathley Damosel*, Kemp Owyne transforms Dove Isabel from a monster back into a human woman by making love to her, which seems to suggest that the redeeming power here is a kind of spiritual virility. It is interesting, however, that the three talismans that allow Kemp Owyne to touch the monster without losing his life are given to him *by* the monster. They do not descend from the Heavenly Father, the world of the celestial masculine power, but seem to have been hidden all along under the monstrous form of the dark feminine power itself. (That the girl's human name is *Dove* Isabel suggests a secret correspondence between her and the Holy Spirit, which in one of Its aspects is precisely the Immanence of God in the natural world.)

This song reminds us of the common practice, in alchemy, of putting apparent impurities—urine, putrefaction, lead, ashes—to spiritual use. If what appears in a fallen state is simply rejected due to its fallenness, no transmutation is possible. If, on the other hand, it is simply accepted on its own level, the same limitation applies. Spiritual power—the Grace of God when well assimilated and freely obeyed—allows us to *engage* with conditions instead of simply accepting or rejecting them. When we encounter the realm of the unredeemed psyche in the early stages of the spiritual Path, at a point where our faith is still weak and where the power of the Spirit seems distant and abstract to us, it often appears as if the psyche itself were helping us, since at this point we can only experience the gifts of the Spirit in terms of their psychic reflections. And, at this preliminary stage, we have no choice but to engage with these reflections, dangerous and ambiguous as they are; we reject them only at our peril. The psyche does indeed contain hidden spiritual potentials, but these potentials can only be awakened by an influx of spiritual power and knowledge from beyond the psychic domain. (The hexagram "Inner Truth" in the *I Ching* tells the story of this.) Once the reality of the Spirit has fully dawned upon us, however (as in the hexagram "The Creative"), then the spiritual potential of the psyche is fully revealed—not as any kind of willful activity, but as pure, virginal receptivity to the Spirit and Its power (as in the hexagram "The Receptive"). In "Kemp Owyne," the psyche of the masculine spiritual hero undergoes a change in proximity to the feminine power; though he is active in approaching the monster, he is also receptive: he receives from her the three *royal* talismans that are properly his own, the powers that she has "stolen" from the Spirit in her fall. These talismans are the three primal powers of the psyche, which only become effective when the psyche submits to the Spirit. The *belt* is self-restraint; the *ring* is loyalty and faithfulness; the *brand* (which could be a torch, a source of light, but is more likely a sword) the power of discrimination. When the willful passions are restrained by asceticism, the affections are gathered and unified; when the affections are unified, the discriminating Intellect awakens. It is this triple conquest that redeems the natural or passional soul, what the Sufis call the *nafs al-ammara,* the "commanding self." But even though Kemp Owyne is protected in his will, his feelings and his mind by the three talismans, if he touches the monster "tail or fin" he will still lose his life. In the struggle to redeem our fallen natural soul, we must guard against becoming fascinated by its subhuman aspects. We must keep our attention fixed upon the human potential it carries within it; only this is deserving of our kiss, and capable of receiving it. If we remain vigilant and do not lose our courage, our soul will be freed from its entanglement in manifest existence and reunited with its spiritual Source. Speaking in terms of masculine psyche in particular, which is the subject of this ballad, if God becomes King of our spiritual heart, then we will become king, and spouse, of our human soul.

The Laily Worm and the Machrel of the Sea

I was but seven year auld
  When my mither she did die;
My father married the ae warst woman
  The warld did ever see.

"For she has made me the laily worm,
  That lies at the fit o the tree,
An my sister Masery she's made
  The Machrel of the Sea.

"An every Saturday at noon
  The Machrel comes to me,
An she takes my laily head
  An lays it on her knee,
She kaims it wi a siller kaim,
  An washes't in the sea.

"Seven knights hae I slain,
  Sin I lay at the fit of the tree,
An ye war na my ain father,
  The eight ane ye should be."

"Sing on your song, ye Laily Worm,
  That ye did sing to me:"
"I never sung that song but what
  I would it sing to thee.

"I was but seven year auld,
  When my mither she did die;
My father married the ae warst woman
  The warld did ever see.

"For she changed me to the Laily Worm,
  That lies at the fit o the tree,
And my sister Masery
  To the Machrel of the Sea.

"And every Saturday at noon
  The Machrel comes to me,

An she takes my laily head
  An lays it on her knee,
An kames it wi a siller kame,
  An washes it i the sea.

"Seven knights hae I slain,
  Sin I lay at the fit o the tree,
An ye war na my ain father,
  The eighth ane ye shoud be."

He sent for his lady,
  As fast as send could he:
"Whar is my son that ye sent frae me,
  And my daughter, Lady Masery?"

"Your son is at our king's court,
  Serving for meat an fee,
An your daughter's at our queen's court,
  . . . . .

"Ye lie, ye ill woman,
  Sae loud as I hear ye lie;
My son's the Laily Worm,
  That lies at the fit o the tree,
And my daughter, Lady Masery,
  Is the Machrel of the Sea!"

She has tane a siller wan,
  An gien him strokes three,
And he has started up the bravest knight
  That ever your eyes did see.

She has taen a small horn,
  An loud an shrill blew she,
An a' the fish came her untill
  But the proud machrel of the sea:
"Ye shapeit me ance an unseemly shape,
  An ye's never mare shape me."

He has sent to the wood

> For whins and for hawthorn,
> An he has taen that gay lady,
> An there he did her burn.

In this ballad as in "Kemp Owyne," the dead mother is the Garden of Eden, or Eve before the fall, and the "warst woman" this fallen world. The father, however, is not quite Adam, or not entirely so. As the hidden spiritual center of the human soul, he is also the *imago dei*—and therefore, by extension, the Presence of the Father, at least in potential.

In "The Laily Worm and the Machrel of the Sea," both the masculine and the feminine powers of the soul are fallen; the "warst women" has here transformed the son of the father into a "laily (loathsome) worm," and his sister into a mackerel. The two children are Adam and Eve in their fallen condition—who, as offspring of the same Heavenly Father, can legitimately be seen as brother and sister. (That the boy is transformed when seven years old indicates the loss of innocence and the beginning of worldliness. In traditional Catholic doctrine, seven is considered to be the "age of reason"; children younger than seven years are believed to be incapable of individual sin and guilt.)

For Adam to be changed into a worm is for him to become earthly and mortal. And for his sister Eve to become transformed into a fish symbolizes the obscurity, slipperiness and elusiveness of the natural world when seen through the eye of a fallen order of human perception. To Adam before the fall the world was a theophany, and the living form of that theophany was Eve, his helpmate. But now, in his fallen condition, the world appears subhuman, hidden in its own secret depths; the "metaphysical transparency of phenomena" has been lost. That the fish is a mackerel, a name which is related to the Latin *maculosus*, "spotted," means that she is no longer spotless, no longer *immaculate*; she has been corrupted by the sin of man. She must wait for the birth of the Virgin Mary, the "immaculate conception," before her receptivity to the Grace of God can begin to be restored. Yet even after the loss of Eden, the natural world is not entirely fallen; the Machrel of the Sea can still serve as helpmate to the Laily Worm by combing his hair with a silver comb and washing it in the sea. Contact with even fallen nature can still purify consciousness, though not in any stable way; the beauty and order of nature can still reflect flashes of a higher Reality, though only imperfectly and intermittently. The metal silver represents spiritual receptivity operating on the mental plane. Silver, the lunar metal of which mirrors can be made, reflects the golden light of the Sun, just as the thinking mind reflects the light of the spiritual Intellect. The comb itself, in its ability to untangle the hair, symbolizes the introduction of order into thought, the kind of order that can legitimately be based on investigation and imitation of the natural world. And the arrival of the Machrel of the Sea each Saturday noon may be a reference to the planet Saturn after which Saturday is named. Saturn's metal is lead, the alchemical symbol of fallen matter, the material world at its furthest point from the Spirit—something like the "Craigy's Sea" of "Kemp Owyne." When Christ harrowed Hell on Holy Saturday, he sank to the darkest and heaviest point of existence, opening even the depths of Hades to the spiritual Light.

The Laily Worm, placed at the foot of the Tree of the Knowledge of Good and Evil, has slain seven knights. This motif will be familiar to readers of Sir James Frazer's *The Golden Bough*, in the person of the King of the Wood of Nemi in Italy, within whose confines lies a lake sacred to the goddess Diana. The King of the Wood was one among those archaic sacred kings who won their kingship by killing their predecessors in ritual battle, and who, standing at the foot of their sacred tree, were required to defend themselves in single combat against rivals for the succession. Frazer relates this tradition to the belief that the fertility of the crops and the integrity of the kingdom were dependent upon the virility of the king. And, as with many other similar remnants of ancient Paganism, this mythic and ritual fragment contains a germ of metaphysical truth. The King of the Wood is Man, the *axis mundi* who connects the natural world to its Divine Source—and as we have seen in our own time, if Man loses his spiritual center, the Earth begins to die. In the words of the Qur'an [33:72] quoted above in the Introduction, "We offered the Trust to the heavens and the earth and the hills, but they shrank from bearing it and were afraid of it. And man assumed it. Lo, he hath proved a tyrant and a fool."

But who are the seven knights slain by the Laily Worm? These may symbolize the seven psycho-physical powers that correspond to the seven planets (in the macrocosm) and the seven *chakras* (in the human microcosm)—and which, since they are still only cosmic elements, aspects of the manifest world but not the Transcendent Source of it, do not possess the power to free the Worm from his cosmic prison, to "slay" him in his fallen nature and return him to his human form. As Christ was resurrected on "the eighth day of the week," showing Him to be beyond the power of the seven planets (for which the seven days of the week are named), so only the Worm's father, only the presence and power of God, can redeem him.

The redemption takes place when the Worm recites to his father, in song, the whole story of his fall. The father is the only listener. And when the recitation is done, he realizes that it is his own son who has become the Laily Worm, and his daughter the Machrel of the Sea; his evil wife has bewitched them. So he confronts her with this knowledge, and she is forced to admit her crime—forced as well to strike him three times with a silver wand (as if in a failed attempt to cast a spell on him), thereby transforming him into a brave young knight. Here we can see how the father is a symbol of *gnosis*, the power to see through the illusions of *Maya* which form the basis of this fallen world. And once *Maya* is unmasked, she is compelled to turn all her power over to the one who has exposed her; she must become his *shakti*. Silver, as the lunar metal, represents the principle of manifestation; by striking the father three times with a silver wand, she brings out into active manifestation (in terms of the three powers of the soul: thought, will and feeling) the power of the hidden God. Divine Manifestation now serves Man, by virtue of the *imago dei*, the Transcendent God within him—which is why, when the evil wife, who is the cosmic Regime of Nature, tries to summon the Machrel of the Sea, she no longer possesses that power. The Machrel defies her regime, denying it the power ever to "shape" her again. The clear implication is that from here on only God can shape her, because now she understands herself not as formed by *Maya*, by the conditioning powers of nature and the influences of the planetary spheres, but by the eternal knowledge of her that is possessed by God alone.

And though this part of the narrative does not appear in the song as it comes down to us, the Laily Worm and the Machrel of the Sea are undoubtedly restored at last to their human forms, and reunited. The evil wife, at any rate—now that whatever spiritual truth and power (as *vidya-maya*) she may once have possessed have returned to their proper role as *shakti* of the human form—is reduced to the dead husk that's left (*avidya-maya*), the husk of pure illusion. As such, she is burned by her husband like the evil witch she is—because illusion, from the standpoint of Absolute Reality, has no right to exist, and in fact does not exist.[1] But why is she burned on a pyre made of *hawthorn* and *whins* (furze or gorse)? According to Robert Graves in *The White Goddess*, the hawthorn is the tree that corresponds to the month of May, sacred to the goddess Maia—who is *Maya*. And furze, the "tree" of the Vernal Equinox, is (according Welsh folklore, as recounted by Graves) "good against witches." But since furze is associated with the beginning of Spring, the implication is that *Maya* never really dies. Purified by fire—the fire of the *Mahapralaya*, the end of the cosmic cycle—she returns again as *vidya-maya*, the manifestation of, and the Path of return to, the Hidden God.

1. The word "witch" today refers to a supposed practitioner of an ancient Pagan religion. But to the actual Pagans of the ancient world, a witch—or someone called by various other names later translated by that word—was a person who spread chaos and destruction through the community by magical means. As a point of ethics, I believe that nobody should be burned by anybody for anything; as a point of information, it is important to realize that the Pagan Druids themselves sometimes burned witches.

7

SCARBOROUGH FAIR

GOD AS SEEKER

Many of my generation first heard the ballad "Scarborough Fair" through the version sung by Simon and Garfunkel (with all those impressionistic, baroque flourishes in the back-text, carrying a vaguely anti-war message). It's interesting how traditional folk ballads made their appearance in the counter-culture of those times, through Buffy St-Marie, Judy Collins, Bob Dylan, and especially Joan Baez. In that context they represented one of the many chaotic and conflicting strands of cultural material that were "liberated" from the collective memory of the West by the social upheavals of the 60's (not the least of which was the advent of LSD). Joan Baez in particular—partly due to the quite obviously *aristocratic* Spanish blood she carries in her veins (with its Arab tributaries), which she invoked to produce her first albums—was able to incarnate, *as artist*, a high romantic spirit that accurately transmitted the deep, spiritual resonances of her material. None of us can really live that way any more (except in secret), but we can allow the romantic spirit of such ballads to awaken aspects of the secret spiritual Heart that seem to be capable of flowering in no other way.

The spiritual romance of "Scarborough Fair," though we usually hear little in it beyond its embroidered "Renaissance Faire" surface, contains a deep spiritual secret. In view of this secret, I have produced a "restored" text based on three less-than-complete versions. The first of these is labeled "[1]" at the end of each stanza; the second, into which I have interpolated material from the first, is labeled "[2]"; and the Simon and Garfunkel version is labeled "[S & G]."

Are you going to Scarborough Fair?
  Parsley, sage, rosemary and thyme
Remember me to one who lives there
  For she once was a true love of mine. [S & G]

Have her make me a cambric shirt
  Parsley, sage, rosemary and thyme
Without a seam or fine needle work
  And then she'll be a true love of mine. [1]

Have her wash it in yonder dry well
  Parsley, sage, rosemary and thyme
Where ne'er a drop of water e'er fell
  And then she'll be a true love of mine. [1]

~~Can you~~ [*Have her*] dry it on yonder thorn,
  Parsley, sage, rosemary and thyme,
Which never bore blossom since Adam was born
  ~~And you shall~~ [*And then she'll*] *be a true lover of mine.* [2]

Tell her to find me an acre of land
  Parsley, sage, rosemary, and thyme
Between the salt water and the sea strand
  Then she'll be a true love of mine [S & G]

Plow the land with the horn of a lamb
  Parsley, sage, rosemary and thyme
Then sow some seeds from north of the dam
  And then she'll be a true love of mine. [1]

~~Can you~~ [*Have her*] reap it with a sickle of leather,
  Parsley, sage, rosemary and thyme,
And bind it up with a peacock's feather?
  And you shall be a true lover of mine. [2]

If she tells me she can't, I'll reply
  Parsley, sage, rosemary and thyme
Let me know that at least she will try
  And then she'll be a true love of mine. [1]

Love imposes impossible tasks

Parsley, sage, rosemary and thyme
Though not more than any heart asks
 And I must know she's a true love of mine. [1]

Dear, when thou hast finished thy task
 Parsley, sage, rosemary and thyme
Come to me, my hand for to ask
 For thou then art a true love of mine. [1]

When you have done and finished your work,
 Parsley, sage, rosemary and thyme,
Then come to me for your cambric shirt,
 And you shall be a true lover of mine. [2]

The pivotal secret of "Scarborough Fair" lies in the answer to the question "who is the singer?" A man asks a traveler on his way to Scarborough Fair to remember him to the one who lives there, because she was once a true love of his, in times past. But he doesn't stop there; he tells the traveler to propose to her a series of seemingly impossible tasks, by the accomplishment of which she will prove her that love for him is *true*.

The answer, and its immediate echoes, are as follows: The singer is God; the traveler is an angel; Scarborough Fair is this world; and *the one who lives there* is the human soul. The soul was once enveloped in God's love, in that timeless time before the world was made; then it fell, or quested, or was sent out into this world, where only by the sweat of its brow could it eat bread. Why?

This "why" is actually one of the thorniest questions in all metaphysics, but rather than writing a whole book about it within what I had hoped would be a fairly short chapter of the present book, I'll restrict my answer to a brief piece of "folk" wisdom: because *absence makes the heart grow fonder.* We think we are seeking God, while all the time it is God Who is seeking us. Our intermittent but ongoing seeking for Him is nothing but His eternal seeking for us, reflected in the mirror of His cosmic manifestation—"in a glass, darkly." We can never reach Him, no matter how long and how hard we try; but by the same token, He has already reached us, from all eternity. He found us before we were born, before we were conceived. Having searched our bowels and our reins in the black night of time, He always knew us, before we even began to know ourselves, when we were nothing but *a twinkle in our mother's eye.*

This world of buying and selling, of bright wares displayed, of good and bad bargains, is a lot like a fair on market day. When we go to the fair, we leave our home and family, our intimate circle, to mix with just anybody; we mingle ourselves with *circumstances,* with whoever or whatever happens to be "standing around." We might get drunk; we might get into fights; we might chase strange women; we might get swindled out of a whole year's work. And worse than all that, we might forget the way back home, and the Name of our True Beloved.

This is why the Singer sings "remember me." God remembers the human soul lost in the wilderness of becoming; He sends reminders to that soul (prophets; angels; sacred scriptures, holy saints) to help it remember Him (cf. the words of the Qur'an, "It is I who have sent down the Remembrance"). Our remembrance of Him, in time, is made possible only by His remembrance of us, in eternity—a remembrance that comes to us in the form of a messenger sent with a letter from our true Beloved, like the one in that beautiful Gnostic fable *The Hymn of the Pearl.* And as we have seen above, the essence of invocatory prayer, and the true purpose of *any* prayer, is first and foremost to help us remember God, and to make that remembrance constant.

Now let us descend (or rather rise) to specifics: The refrain of "Scarborough Fair" is "parsley, sage, rosemary and thyme." Looking up the symbolic meaning of these herbs in *A Modern Herbal* (1931) by Mrs. M. Grieve, I find that *parsley* symbolizes death (there being plenty of poisonous herbs in the parsley family, like fool's parsley and poison hemlock); *sage,* salvation (the genus *salvia*); *rosemary,* memory ("There's rosemary for memory" says Hamlet to Ophelia); and *thyme,* courage.

Death, salvation, memory and courage are the four powers, or virtues, necessary to travel the spiritual Path. Parsley symbolizes the death of the ego ("He who loses his life, for My sake, shall find it"); Sage is salvation through the Grace of God, the one necessity on the Path that we can't provide for ourselves, but is freely given (though to assimilate it and make it effective in our lives takes serious work). These two make up the vertical or *transpersonal* axis of the Cross, the one active (self-annihilation, at the base) and the other passive (receptivity to Grace, at the crown). Both death and salvation transcend the psyche; they are properly powers of the Spirit.

The other two virtues have to do not with the Spirit *per se* but with the psyche's obedient response to the Spirit; as such they make up the horizontal axis of the Cross. Rosemary is memory in the sense of the Sufi practice of *dhikr* (remembrance) or the Hesychast *mnimi Theou* (remembrance of God). Memory in this sense is not nostalgic reverie but rather faithful constancy in keeping one's mind fixed on an unseen Reality, as if on the image of one's distant Beloved who is traveling in a foreign land—"the Presence of things hoped for, the Evidence of things not seen." (Songs of the lover faithful to the distant beloved, like "John Riley," though they are set on the human level, draw their ultimate power from the relationship between the soul and God—as do all human relationships, if the truth be told. When the bond between the soul and God is broken, then "Things fall apart; the center cannot hold.") Rosemary (*rosmarinus*, "sea dew" or "sea rose") is sacred to the Virgin Mary, whose name is related to the Latin *mare*, "sea." Roses have always been associated with the Virgin, as they were with the goddess Aphrodite before her; Marian apparitions are often accompanied by a preternatural scent of roses. And her connection with rosemary as symbolic of spiritual memory confirms her as the patroness of invocatory prayer.

As for the identification of thyme with martial courage in the context of the spiritual Path, this is what St. Paul was talking about when he said "I have completed the race, I have fought the good fight"; (the same idea is expressed in the spiritual "King Jesus": "Ride on, King Jesus/No man can hinder me"). Thyme symbolizes the fighting spirit necessary to travel the Path without being frightened or distracted or lured away from the constant remembrance of God; according to *A Modern Herbal*, knights going into battle would sometimes wear sprigs of thyme for courage. *Thymos* in Greek denotes a kind of life force associated with passion and aggression, similar to the Hindu *rajas*, one of the three *gunas* or modes of *prakriti,* the primal cosmic substance. *Rajas* is the cosmic expansive power that expresses itself through warriors and kings. (*Thymos,* however, is perhaps related, analogically, poetically, or "synchronistically"—according to *nirukta,* that is, not according to etymology—to the Sanskrit *tamas,* another of the *gunas,* denoting the sinking and contracting power. Inversions like this are fairly common; for example, the *devas* are gods to the Hindus but demons [*daevas*] to the Zoroastrians; the *ashuras* are gods to the Zoroastrians but demons [*asuras*] to the Hindus. The Greeks, at one point, may well have conceived of the battle-fury of kings as a dark, earthly, *chthonic* power—like the *duende.*) In terms of Hesychast spirituality, *thymos* is sometimes translated as "the incensive faculty." When applied to the spiritual Path, it is the power to "be angry with anger," to forcibly repel evil and temptation. Memory is receptive, so let's place it on the feminine or left-hand arm of the Cross. Courage is active; it belongs on the masculine, right-hand arm. (Remembrance is *essentially* feminine, not personally so; real women need courage as much as men do. And courage is only essentially masculine; real men also need to *remember*—to see beyond the world of action to the world of Being. Remembrance is of a man's feminine soul, which is why Divine Wisdom appears in the form of Sophia, as Beatrice appeared to Dante. And true courage is of a women's masculine, spiritual soul; this courageous soul is the very Hero that will save her.) Remembrance of God is essentially receptive, yet it needs courage in order to become a constant practice, whatever the uncertainties of life or the turbulence of the psyche may throw our way. Courage, on the other hand—the "unseen warfare," the "greater *jihad,*" the war against the passional soul, against everything that would distract us from the Remembrance—is nothing if not active. Yet if it is cut off from that dimension of things where the Good we fight to attain already exists in its eternal perfection, spiritual courage will degenerate into the egotism of self-will, and the Remembrance will be lost; the Knight fighting to save the Princess from the Dragon will turn into the Dragon himself.

In "Scarborough Fair" the lover has to complete several impossible tasks in order to win her Beloved. Lots of myths and especially fairy tales include such seemingly impossible tasks. For the soul to reach God on its own knowledge and power is impossible—God must reach it first. Theologically speaking, Grace is a free gift; our work is basically to assimilate that Grace. Without God's Grace, the task is impossible; with it, the work is already done. And as tiny human beings struggling with the immense reality of God, we confront a situation where (mysteriously, and mercifully) the impossible and the inevitable are one.

> Have her make me a cambric shirt
>   Parsley, sage, rosemary and thyme
> Without a seam or fine needle work
>   And then she'll be a true love of mine.

What is this "cambric shirt / Without a seam or fine needle work" which will make its maker a "true love of mine"? *Cambric* is the fine white linen cloth woven at Cambrai in France. Its whiteness is its purity. In classical antiquity candidates for spiritual initiation were generally dressed in white, as in some river baptisms in contemporary Appalachia, where the candidate goes down to the river dressed in his or her own white shroud—because initiation is always a death, and always a resurrection. *Candidatus* in Latin means "dressed in white"; the *candidate* for initiation, unlike those political hucksters who have usurped the name in our own times, must be *candid*: pure of all self-will, hidden agendas, and deceit. In alchemy, this is the fruit of the *albedo*, the "whitening." And the shirt is *seamless* because—like Christ's seamless undergarment that the Roman soldiers cast lots for after He was stripped for crucifixion—it symbolizes *unity of soul*. We can only be worthy of spiritual initiation when we present ourselves as exactly who and what we are, when our mind, our will and our feelings are seamlessly united: only then are we truly candid. (It was never recorded that any single soldier won Jesus' seamless garment in that game— what fragmentary, self-willed impulse of the fallen soul, ruled by uncertain fate and all its games of chance, could put on the soul of absolute unity and purity?) As revealed in this first stanza of "Scarborough Fair," unity of soul, on whatever spiritual level we actually occupy, high or low, is the necessary first step on the spiritual Path.

> Have her wash it in yonder dry well
>   Parsley, sage, rosemary and thyme
> Where ne'er a drop of water e'er fell
>   And then she'll be a true love of mine.

Candidness (for none of us can equal Jesus in this) is a level of purity that calls for and initiates a further purification. To wash one's soul in the water of a dry well is to attain what the Hesychasts call *apatheia* (dispassion) and the Sufis *sahw* (sobriety); as the pre-Socratic philosopher Heraclitus said, "dry souls are best." It is indeed purifying and refreshing like water, but totally free of *soddenness*, of the worldly drunkenness and sentimentality that so often masquerades as the wine of the Holy Spirit. Nikitas Stithatos, in *The Philokalia*, calls it a "life-quickening deadness." Perhaps the best sensual symbol for it is the taste of water itself.

> ~~Can you~~ [*Have her*] dry it on yonder thorn,
>   Parsley, sage, rosemary and thyme,
> Which never bore blossom since Adam was born
>   ~~And you shall~~ [*And then she'll*] be a true lover of mine.

To dry one's soul on a thorn-tree is gain the capacity to suffer the thorn of God's Majesty in quest for the blossom of His Beauty, and to know that Beauty and that Majesty as One. It is to come into the magnetic field of the *axis mundi*, the Tree of Life—here undoubtedly represented by, or deliberately suggesting, the Glastonbury Thorn, in close proximity to which "England's Green and Pleasant Land" (for those with eyes to see) is transformed into the Earthly Paradise. If the thorn never bore blossom since Adam was born, then Adam *was* that blossom, the outermost expression of the Divine Center in this material world, as any of us might be if we were to attain the Station of the Thorn Tree—for to return to the Tree of Life is to be restored to the Adamic state, the state of humanity before the Fall.

> Tell her to find me an acre of land
>   Parsley, sage, rosemary, and thyme
> Between the salt water and the sea strand
>   Then she'll be a true love of mine

What exactly is "An acre of land / Between the salt water and the *sea strand*" (the shore)? A piece of land between the land and the sea is certainly a mysterious place. The *land* undoubtedly symbolizes this world and the *sea* the next world, as we have already seen in "The Wife of Usher's Well." But the Sufis, and mystics in general, seek neither the goods of this world nor the reward for good deeds in the future life; they seek God Himself in this present moment. So the acre of land between this world and the next would be the "Paradise of the Essence," God as He is in Himself, not as He is veiled by this world or revealed by the next. The doorway to this Paradise, in Sufi terms, is the *waqt*, the present moment of spiritual time, which lies between past and future, between the solid land of what is already formed and established, and the shifting sea of what *might* be. And the purchase price for this priceless and immeasurable acre of land is—oneself.

> Plow the land with the horn of a lamb
>   Parsley, sage, rosemary and thyme
> Then sow some seeds from north of the dam
>   And then she'll be a true love of mine.

The horn of the Lamb is the power of Christ, the power of self-sacrifice and submission to God's will. Only such perfect submission can plough the hard-baked soil of the spiritual Heart, and make it receptive to the Holy Word. The dam is, again, the barrier between this world and the next, the wall that holds back the Ocean of Infinity, preventing it from flooding this world of earthly limits and dissolving it all back into the Formless Absolute—because if Infinity were to exclude anything, even form and limitation, it would not be truly Infinite. The spiritual Path does not ask us to lose the forms of our souls and our lives in the Divine Infinity (that way lies madness), but requires that we plant the seeds of that Infinity *within* these very forms [see the Parable of the Sower in Matthew 13:3–9; 18–23]. As God said through the mouth of Muhammad, "heaven and earth cannot contain Me, but the heart of my willing slave can contain Me." And the land *north* of the dam is, again, the land of Hyperborea [see Chapter One]. Hyperborea is the realm of *Ursa Major* and *Ursa Minor*, the constellations of the Bears surrounding the north star; and the identification of "north of the dam" with the celestial Hyperborea (see Chapter One) is supported by the fact that in "Are You Going to the Fair?," a New England variant of "Scarborough Fair," the plowing is to be done not with "the horn of a lamb" but "the horn of a bear."

> Can you [*Have her*] reap it with a sickle of leather,
>   Parsley, sage, rosemary and thyme,
> And bind it up with a peacock's feather
>   And you [*she*] shall be a true lover of mine.

In Genesis 3:21, God made "garments of skin" for Adam and Eve after the Fall; according to the Greek Fathers, these garments represent our gross, material bodies. In our garments of skin, exiled from the Axial North to the East of Eden, which is this lower world, only by the sweat of our face shall we eat bread. Life in this world is tough, like leather. And given that life is hard, we'd better make the most of it; we'd better learn how to turn our limitations into tools. If we can pick up the toughness of life and use it like a tool, then we are no longer entirely bound by it. The sickle by which we are called upon to reap the harvest of our spiritual labors is crescent-shaped, like the Moon; everything below the sphere of the Moon, the entire "sublunary" world, is ruled by the cycles of birth and death, symbolized by the lunar phases. Leather is dead skin; we are called to strip off the garments of skin we assumed after the Fall, our tough, materialistic hides, to rise above the cycles of nature, and thereby emerge from the chrysalis of death. The peacock, whose tail-feather binds our sheaves, recollecting them and gathering them together like the scattered limbs of Osiris (the harvested grain) is a symbol of the Resurrection. When we reap our harvest with a leather sickle, our corn is not returned to the ongoing cycles of nature, but gathered instead into the barns of Eternity, where moth and rust cannot corrupt it. (According to *nirukta* we can hear a consonance of meaning between *circle/cycle* and *sickle*, which is shaped like a half-circle. *Sickle* comes from the Latin *secula*, from the verb *secare*, to cut, to section. It is undoubtedly related to *saeculum* or *seculum*, "age," a word which is sometimes used to refer to the age of a man, the *cycle* of his life. If a circle is cut into four quarters it becomes a cycle, like the cycle of the seasons; an aeon becomes a cycle when cut into four ages. It only takes one little cut, as through the stem of an apple, to bring the whole thing crashing down; this *secular* world moves in cycles of "vain repetition" because it is cut off from Eternity.)

Here, after experiencing the exaltation of spiritual understanding, we must still return to the hard facts of life; the time has come for us to die to the world and to ourselves, definitively: This ultimate act of humility, like Christ's submission to His crucifixion, is the only thing that will allow us to reap the fruits of our former labors. All our work on the spiritual Path will be as nothing unless we die, and rise, with Him.

> If she tells me she can't, I'll reply
> Parsley, sage, rosemary and thyme
> Let me know that at least she will try
> And then she'll be a true love of mine.

Willingness and obedience are required on our part; godlike power is not. In the words of Frithjof Schuon:

All great spiritual experiences agree in this: that there is no common measure between the means put into operation and the result. "With men this is impossible, but with God all things are possible," says the Gospel. In fact, what separates man from divine Reality is the slightest of barriers: God is infinitely close to man, but man is infinitely far from God. This barrier, for man, is a mountain; man must stand in front of a mountain which he must remove with his own hands. He digs away the earth, but in vain, the mountain remains; man however goes on digging, in the name of God. And the mountain vanishes. It was never there.[1]

> Love imposes impossible tasks
> Parsley, sage, rosemary and thyme
> Though not more than any heart asks
> And I must know she's a true love of mine.

True! Love alone can turn the pain of love into the deepest expression of love, and thus overcome it. If we believe that the spiri-

1. *Stations of Wisdom* (Bloomington, IN: World Wisdom Books, 1995), p157.

tual struggles we must face have been imposed by a cruel God or an indifferent fate, we will never find the way out of their labyrinth. But if we realize that love always asks, and *must* ask, to be tested by fire, then the willingness necessary to walk the spiritual Path has been found. God has a right to test us, to prove that we love Him. He does not impose these tests upon us in order to learn something He doesn't already know, but to give us the incomparable opportunity of proving our love for Him by our willingness to suffer. From one point of view, it is precisely for this reason we were born into this world.

> Dear, when thou hast finished thy task
>   Parsley, sage, rosemary and thyme
> Come to me, my hand for to ask
>   For thou then art a true love of mine.

On the horizontal axis of the Cross, this is the *coniunctio oppositorum*, the union of opposites, of male and female; on the vertical axis, it is the union of the soul with God, the sacred marriage, the wedding feast of the Lamb.

> When you have done and finished your work,
>   Parsley, sage, rosemary and thyme,
> Then come to me for your cambric shirt,
>   And you shall be a true lover of mine.

Here we see how the *cambric shirt* is both the first step on the spiritual Path and its final end. The Path is hard work, but this work both begins and ends with the free gift of God's Grace. Paradoxically, a purified and unified soul is both the necessary precondition for spiritual progress and the final fruit of it; as the Zen people say, "in order to be enlightened, first you have to be enlightened." And it is very often true that God, in His mercy, will give the spiritual aspirant at the very beginning a free foretaste of final victory, to forearm him against the rigors of the Path and keep him from losing hope.

In one sense, the seamless, finished and purified shirt has been sent ahead, once completed, from Scarborough Fair to the heavenly worlds; in another sense, it was already there. Our immortal soul, our eternal garment, the contrary of this garment of skin, has in one sense been with God all along. The Zoroastrians speak of each one of us as having a *fravashi*, our eternal counterpart or "soul-mate" who never fell, like we did, into this lower world; at the end of the spiritual Path, as at the end of a life well lived, we are reunited with her. *The Hymn of the Pearl*, which contains a Gnostic rendition of originally Zoroastrian material, presents this celestial counterpart as a "robe of glory," opposing it to the "impure garment of Egypt"— the garment of skin. Every fall is a fall from Reality into illusion— which necessarily means that, in *one* sense, it never really happened. We may wander into illusion and suffer all the terrible consequences of it, but God, Who created us, is totally free of illusion: and there is no imperfection in His work.

AFTERWORD

As I have done my best to demonstrate in this book, when we open our mouths to speak we are drawing upon a vast metaphysical lore-hoard of incredible richness and depth that stretches back to the dawn of human history. We are largely unaware of this. Just as we habitually live on the outer surface of our own lives, so we tend to walk only on the surface of our language. Words, to us, are mostly utilitarian. They are useful for various worldly transactions, though sometimes we will allow our speech to rise as far as humor, or levity. But beyond levity is wit, and beyond wit, wisdom. Our words are wiser than we are; our languages are woven on the golden loom of an eternal, celestial knowledge that dwells beyond the world of earthly humanity. This truth is attested to by the myths and religious doctrines of all peoples, which declare that language is not a human construction, but a miracle, a gift of God: "In the beginning was the Word."

But where our daily speech is merely utilitarian, the concentrated and "crystallized" language of true poetry, like that of scripture and divine liturgy, can give us glimpses of higher realities. And if we are willing to labor and sacrifice to conform ourselves to these glimpses, and also possess the *science* of this conformation, a science known as "religion," then these flashes of insight (God willing) will be transformed into solid realizations that neither the sorrows of life nor the wiles of the enemy can ever take away from us.

The art of poetry has fallen to so low an estate in our times that the dread words "let me just read you this poem I wrote, don't worry it's not that long" will produce immense discomfort in those unlucky enough to be within earshot, resulting in hurried glances at wristwatches (real or imagined), mumbled excuses and sudden memories of seriously pressing engagements. This is because, just as the Devil is now the prince of this world that God created, so the ego is now the prince of poetry. When individual self-expression first broke off from the traditional mythopoeia of the human race, it produced flashes of real brilliance—but it also separated the human word from the Word of God, ultimately resulting in a withering of man's intelligence, coupled with a drying-up of the natural affections, such as was predicted in the Epistle of Timothy as a sign of the End Times. Consequently, if there is any way back to at least a partial recollection of the lost Word now scattered and dissipated in the passions of this world, it will be through a study of those artifacts of human language that do not lie under the dark and oppressive sign of individual self-expression. And since poetry in its original form and stature was never separated from song (just as song was rarely separated from dance), one of the best places to carry on this search is the realm of folk song, and the traditional arts in general.

By "traditional" I mean "non-" or "pre-individual." As Ezra Pound pointed out, the exquisite architecture and stone-carving of the medieval cathedrals was sometimes signed *Adamo me fecit*: "Adam made me." In other words, some of the greatest works of medieval art were left deliberately unsigned. The cathedrals were not built by some individual genius—like Frank Lloyd Wright, whose homes, those "cathedrals" dedicated to Promethean modernism, are hard to sell nowadays because, though they are sometimes magnificent in a pretentious way, they aren't really pretty, besides having bad roofs and too many windows. The cathedrals of Christendom were built by *Adam*—that is, by Man. Man *is* the temple; who but Man would know how to build it, and build it right?

When we look at a traditional Eastern Orthodox icon, either ancient or contemporary, we see exactly what a "trans-individual" work of art is. In the history of religious art in Italy, we can trace a line from the Byzantine mosaics of Ravenna, through the works of Giotto and Cimabue, to the "high Renaissance" paintings of Titian, Botticelli, Leonardo, Raphael, and Michelangelo. The Byzantine mosaics are trans-individual; Giotto and Cimabue are at the precise tuning-point between the trans-individual and the individual or psychological treatment of their subjects; the works of the later masters, though they are luminous in their physical and psychic beauty, have lost their spiritual center. All questions of individual taste aside, it can't be denied that traditional Byzantine iconography is on a higher level *ontologically* than the works of the Renaissance masters. Preternatural steams of myrrh and miraculous healings are attributed to icons, like the myrrh-streaming icon of Jesus' grandma St. Anna my wife and I recently venerated in Louisville, which was painted only a few years ago. They are not attributed to the Mona Lisa.

And traditional folk songs are trans-individual in exactly the same sense as an icon or a cathedral. The singer is not really Jean Ritchie or Pete Seeger; the singer is Orpheus—the archaic Greek demigod who symbolizes the human form divinely endowed with speech, and whose function in the cosmic order is to mediate between the high intellectual light of Apollo above and the deep passionate emotion of Dionysius beneath—between (in Lorca's terms) the *angel* and the *duende*. In terms of the roots of both music and poetry in the western world, this is the original conception of Man—undoubtedly descended from that ancient and nameless First Shaman and his colleagues, who went into deep trance singing his spirit-songs, who rose to meet God in the heavens above or went down to fight demons the underworlds below, seated on his flying drum. (My friend Barry McDonald pointed out to me one of the "shamanic" qualities of old-time mountain singing: how the high, penetrating nasal timbre of certain notes can actually *crack the shell of this world*. Notes like that are not *produced* by the voice but *found* by it. The note is always there, hidden in the silence. The voice rises to the level of that eternal note, then disappears inside it; it's only then that the note actually reaches our ears.) The song and language of the shaman were "utilitarian" as well, but in the *theurgic* sense, not the psychological or commercial one. The use of his art was to heal the sick, to track the motions of the animal herds, to bring the life-giving rain. His language did not exist to let him express himself, but to empower him serve his people.

When we sing traditional folk songs, we are standing partly in that lineage; we are carrying forward into these extremely late times a tiny portion of world-sustaining power of the first great Songs of the human race. And the only way we can transmit this power is to *get out of our own way*. (Anybody who compares the traditional songs of the Carter Family, for example, to songs by many of the glitzy country singers of the present day will hear exactly what I mean.) We do not first *compose* folk songs—we *hear* them. And if we really want to hear them, we will have to learn, in the words of Lew Welch from his poem "Wobbly Rock," how to "sit real still and keep your mouth shut." We are only the vehicles of music (and of life too), not the owners of it.

If we really know this, then we can sing.

APPENDIX

A VINDICATION OF MY METHOD

SINCE MY HERMENEUTIC has a lot to do with the inner, inherent, or *eternal* meanings of words—meanings that can't always be discovered through etymology, with its sense of word derivations as based on their history alone—I need to say something about my method in this regard. As was mentioned above, I sometimes like to look at words in terms the Hindu science of *nirukta*. As a poet and metaphysician, it is my usual practice to deal with philology more in terms of *nirukta* than of etymology; you might say that I approach my material more like a crystallographer than an historian.

While I was writing this book my method was challenged by a competent scholar, who asked me three very good questions: (1) "How can you determine which variant of a song is the original, or closest to the original, without presenting detailed histories of the songs you are dealing with, which in many cases are not available?" (2) "How can you claim that words that only sound alike are actually related in terms of meaning when etymology demonstrates that they are apparently derive from different antecedents? For example, you claim that the Hindu *tamas* [heaviness, obscurity, the sinking force] and the Greek *thymos* [aggression; battle-fury] are related— yet according to the etymologists, the former seems to derive from a root *temh-*, reflected by such other words as English *dim*; while the latter goes back to a *dheu(m)*, which has resulted in Latin *fumus* [smoke] and the broadly synonymous Sanskrit *dhuma*." And, (3) "How can you claim to know the *real* meaning of a folk song when every song has so many variants? How can you prove that you are not simply reading into a given song the meaning you wish to find there? One can't simply say that an interpretation is vindicated by the fact that it makes sense." I answered him in this wise:

(1) The truest version is the one that is the most unified, the most intelligible and the most complete, and therefore the most beautiful. And if a conflation of several versions produces a song that is more unified, more intelligible or more complete than any single version, then that song is truer still. Such a version will be the closest of all to its Original—by which I mean its archetype, not necessarily its earliest historical version. Since all spiritual traditions descend from eternity into time, after which they become subject to entropy and degeneration, historically earlier versions of a song will tend to be closer to the Original than later ones; nonetheless, the most unified, intelligible and complete version of a given song is still the truest one, no matter how early or late it may have appeared. Given that a comprehensive history of the various versions of a particular song is by and large impossible to produce, since folk songs are transmitted mostly by oral tradition, we are reduced—or as I would rather say, exalted—to a quest for eternal precedents, not temporal antecedents.

(2) The Hindu science of *nirukta* is the art of discerning what we would probably nowadays call *poetic* analogies in words that sound the same or have a similar structure, apart from their etymological derivations. Applying this science to the example you provided, given that *temh-* and *dhuma* obviously sound alike, I need only point out that what is *smoky* is often also *dim*: similarity of sound, here, is paralleled by consonance of meaning. Poetically considered, *tamas* is a dim, smoky, smoldering obscurity—one that is susceptible to eruption as *thymos*, just as sullen depression may easily erupt into anger and violence.

In that vast and ancient pre-literate age, before the cranes of language were shot and hung as letters, similarity in sound was immediately recognized as representing similarity in meaning. This consonance between *melopoeia* (the sounds of words) and *logopoeia* (their meanings) allowed human language to indicate, as if by triangulation, objective realities both comprising and transcending the sensual domain, thereby demonstrating an *intrinsic* and *organic* relationship between words and the objects they signify. The words denoting things (and therefore invoking them) were not simply conventional ways of referring to those things, but were understood to be their *real names*—which is why it is still possible to say, in terms of sacred languages such as Hebrew, Arabic and Sanskrit, that "God and His Name are One." The name of a thing is the *sacrament* of it, "the outward and visible sign of [the real presence of] an inward grace [or true, objective form]." Adam could name the animals (in Genesis) and the angels (in the Qur'an) because, being formed in the Image of God, he knew their real names already—which were equally God's Names—since he was in fact *composed* of them, "fearfully and wonderfully made."

In the case of Arabic, we can see the remnant of this earlier, more comprehensive quality of human language in the fact that most or all of the words stemming from the same tri-literal root have meanings that are *poetically* analogous. This adds a dimension of depth and compacted meaning to Arabic poetry that is impossible in English, where what remains of such verbal analogies is usually reduced to the lowest form of humor, namely the *pun*. *Nirukta* is seen by modern etymologists as a kind of spurious or folk etymology, or at best a sort of punning. But given that 'punning' on the analogies between words that are similar in sound has been going on for many thousands of years—an art which only poets seem to have preserved down to our own times, at least in the West—then there is no way to separate spurious or folk etymology from the 'real thing'. And since poetry came before prose, and since—as Owen Barfield has demonstrated—earlier ages thought much more poetically, analogically, transcendentally and *concretely* than we do today, we can safely say that folk etymology, or *nirukta*, being of truly ancient pedigree, is woven into the very fabric of language itself, and draws its legitimacy directly from this fact. The word 'Sufi', for example, has been etymologically derived from the Arabic words for 'purity' (*safa*) or 'wool' (*swf*)—yet from the standpoint of *nirukta*, it also resonates with the Greek word for 'wisdom' (*sophia*) and the Aramaic for 'reed' (*suf*)—given that the 'unlettered' Prophet Muhammad, peace and blessings be upon him, can be seen as a hollow reed who spoke only when the Breath of the Merciful blew through him. It is probably impossible, in etymological terms, to show a common ancestor of all these words; in terms of poetic analogy, however, they are strictly *consonant*. The early Muslim mystics who chose SUF for their title may well have been consciously pun-ning on all these languages, since some were undoubtedly conver-sant with every one of them; or the word might have been a direct inspiration from God that accomplished the same sort of calling-together of many meanings, quite apart from their conscious knowledge or the lack of it. (The discernment of such analogies between otherwise unrelated words was probably not considered 'funny' in ancient times, but was rather recognized as an element of piety, intellection and spiritual imagination. *Finnegan's Wake* is the tomb of language, not the womb of it, though tomb and womb do have certain elements in common.)

My way of investigating and expressing the meanings of words is precisely set down by Ananda K. Coomaraswamy in his essay 'Nirukta = Hermeneia' [*Coomaraswamy, Selected Papers: Metaphys-ics*; Bollingen Series LXXXIX, Princeton: Princeton Univ. Press, 1977, ed. Roger Lipsey]:

> The assumption more immediately underlying the traditional science of hermeneutics (*nirukta*) is that there remains in spoken language a trace of universality, and particularly of natural *mimesis* (by which, of course, we do not mean a merely onomo-topoetic likeness but one of true analogy); that even in languages considerably modified by art and convention, there still survives a considerable part of naturally adequate symbolism. It is assumed, in other words, that certain assonances, which may or may not correspond to the actual pedigrees of words, are never-theless indications of their affinities and meanings, just as we recognize family likeness, of both appearance and character, apart from the line of direct inheritance. All of which is anything but a matter of 'folk etymology'; it is a matter not of etymology at all in the narrowest sense of the word, but rather of significant assonance, and in any case the 'folk' tradition is a matter of 'folk' only in respect to its transmission, not its origin; 'folklore' and Philosophia Perennis spring from a common source. . . . [pp 261–262]

Plato employ[s] the hermeneutic method in the Cratylus—for example, when he says, "'to have called' (τὸ καλέσαν) things useful is one and the same thing as to speak of 'the beautiful' (τὸ καλόν)"... throughout this dialogue he is dealing with the problem of the nature of the relation between sounds and meanings, inquiring whether this is an essential or an accidental one. The general conclusion is that the true name of anything is that which has a natural (Skt. *sahaja*) meaning—i.e., is really an "imitation" (μίμησις) of the thing itself in terms of sound, just as in a painting things are 'imitated' in terms of color—but that because of the actual imperfection of vocal imitation, which may be thought of as a matter of inadequate recollection, the formation of words in use has been helped out by art and their meaning partly determined by convention. What is meant by natural meaning can be understood when we find that Socrates and Cratylus are represented as agreeing that "the letter *rho* ... is expressive of rapidity, motion and hardness." [pp 257–258]

One thus begins to glimpse a theory of expression in which ideation, denomination and individual existence are inseparable aspects, conceptually distinguishable when objectively considered, but coincident in the subject. What this amounts to is the concept of a single living language, not knowable in its entirety by any individual principle but in itself the sum of all imaginable articulations, and in the same way corresponding to all imaginable acts of being: the "Spoken Word" of God is consequently "the sum of all language" (*vācikam sarvaṇmayam; Abhinaya Darpaṇa* 1). All existing languages are partially remembered and more or less fragmented echoes of this universal tongue, just as all modes of vision are more or less obscure refractions of the world-picture (*jagaccitra; Svātmanirūpaṇa* 95) or eternal mirror (Augustine, *De Civitate Dei* xɪɪ.29) which, if one knew and saw in their entirety and simultaneity, would be to be omniscient.... [p 260]

The metaphysical doctrine of a universal language is ... by no means to be thought of as asserting that a universal language was ever actually spoken by any people under the sun; the metaphysical concept of a universal speech is, in fact, the conception of a single sound [p 261]—[i.e., the *Omkara*, the *Logos*, the Word that was (and is) in the beginning].

Coomaraswamy refers to René Guénon's drawing of an analogy

between *Agni* (the Hindu god of fire, etymologically related to the Latin *ignis*) and the Latin *Angus* ('lamb', an epithet of Christ) as an example of *nirukta* operating beyond the borders of a single language. Elsewhere [p78] he says:

> That the human body is called "a city of God (*puram ... brahm-nah*, AV [*Atharva Veda*] x.2.28; *brahmapura, passim*)" is well known; and he who is a bird (*pakṣī bhūtvā*) [who] becomes a citizen in all these cities (*sarvāsu pūrṣu puriśayaḥ*) is hermeneutically *purusa* (BU [*Brhadaranyaka Upanishad*] II.5.18),

and includes as a note [n48]

> Just as also for Plato, man is a "body politic" ($\pi \acute{o} \lambda \iota \varsigma$ = *pur*).

I would add that *purusa* or *purusha* sounds almost the same and has almost exactly the same meaning as the English word *person*. Etymologically, however, *person* is derived from the Latin word *persona*, denoting a 'mask' as something which is 'sounded-through'. *Poetically*, nonetheless, we have every right to speak of a 'polis' or a 'body politic' as the outer mask of a Great Person who speaks through many mouths, but with one voice: *vox populi, vox Dei.*

(3) I nowhere claim that my exegesis of a song is its *only* true meaning. The meaning compacted within true symbols is inexhaustible, which means that any number of exegeses of a given symbol can be equally true. Hermeneutic meaning, to me, is not something which closes accounts with reality, encapsulating a symbol in a single unchanging interpretation, but a power that opens the Creative Imagination to the *Nous* from which it springs, to meaning after meaning, to meanings without end. Of course many attributed meanings are simply wrong because they are poetically impossible, and thus dissonant both with the symbol and with each other. Exegeses that are poetically *consonant*, on the other hand, truly search and research and amplify and plumb the meanings that are objectively there in the symbols they treat. Exegeses that differ in their conclusions will seem to be contradictory only if we assume that only one of them can be true; but if we understand that true symbols are *polyvalent*, we will also understand that more than one exegesis (though certainly not all) can be true, and that all true

symbolic exegeses will be poetically or symbolically *consonant* with each other, whereas all false exegeses will be *dissonant*, both with each other and with the symbol they purport to explain. Exegesis, like poetry, is an imaginative art; consequently no one particular exegesis refutes another, though it may surpass it in unity, intelligibility and completeness. One poem does not refute another, any more than a lion refutes an ox (though he certainly may *eat* him). Exegeses are inexhaustible like the symbols they draw upon; the only difference is that exegeses operate in multiple and analytic mode, symbols in multidimensional and synthetic mode. And to the accusation that I have found what I wanted to find in the songs I have claimed to explicate, I plead guilty, but do so without shame. Certainly I found what I *wanted* to find, which is *meaning*; and what I found is validated, in my opinion, by its unity, its intelligibility and its completeness. A *true* mirror is one which reflects a complete and undistorted image. I called upon these songs to tell me their secrets, and because they knew I could understand those secrets, they complied; they could *hear me listening*. I did not read what I found *into* these songs, but *out of* them. And just because my exegesis of a particular work may differ from another's, the conclusion that it is therefore merely subjective is not justified; I have simply tapped a different and unique aspect of a single, common, objective meaning.

Nonetheless, the question remains: Who put that meaning into those songs? It could only have been put there by individuals both skilled in expression and aware of what they were expressing. Folk traditions are not carried on through some vague group dream, but by particular, individual, conscious artists, albeit anonymous ones. Guénon is undoubtedly right that the first versions of many 'folk' songs and tales, among those that are fully realized as mythopoeia and therefore unified, intelligible and complete, had to have been composed by initiates of the Mysteries. But it is also clear, as Jean Ritchie confirmed to me, that inspiration is not limited to the original authors, but may descend at any point in the life-span of the tradition in question (though such descents will be progressively fewer in the latter days of it); horizontal transmission (memory) is always supplemented and renewed by vertical influx (inspiration). And though symbols may be inexhaustible in essence—just as the Sun never empties itself of light—works of art capable of being explicated in terms of spiritual lore by exegeses that make sense, ones that on their own less-comprehensive level are every bit as unified, intelligible and complete as their originals, had to have been wrought, at least originally, by fully-informed and conscious individuals. The deliberately-chosen limitation that is human art produces works that may still be validly interpreted in more than one way, but because such limitation is inseparable from human intent, the spectrum of valid exegeses of a given work of art will triangulate, and converge, not upon the transcendental inexhaustibility of universal symbols alone, but also upon what one particular man or woman actually meant to say, even though the symbols he or she employed—given that all symbols are Names of God—will have a lot more to say than that.

In the last analysis, the interpretations I have produced are vindicated precisely *because* they make sense: what else *makes sense* as a criterion of interpretation? What I wanted to find in the songs I have explicated is the story of God, and of the spiritual Path by which He may be loved, and known. And if I was able to find Him there, in the meanings I dis-covered, it is because *God is meaning Itself*—the implication being that *every* story—essentially, ultimately, in the final analysis, at the End of the Day—is a story about God. And because every story is really about God, the interpretation of a given story in terms of God—if, that is, it is poetically possible to so interpret it, which in very many cases it is not—is always the truest one; this, in essence, is a re-stating of the doctrine of the Immanence of God in terms of human language. Stories, songs, poems that are the most fully realized mythopoetically, and therefore the most transparent metaphysically—works that are unified, intelligible, complete, and therefore beautiful—reveal this truth. Stories that are less fully realized, and therefore relatively fragmented, obscure, incomplete and ugly, obscure it. But that fragmentation will not last forever. As sundown approaches, God will harvest the meanings of all things and gather them into His barns; whatever was done and known in secret, in obscurity, will be cried from the rooftops. When the threshing is done, all the dodder, the bindweed and the devil's-guts, along with the husks of the good grain, will be burned; the sparks hidden within them for so long will be returned to the One Fire. Creation is composition: apocalypse is exegesis.

Lightning Source UK Ltd.
Milton Keynes UK
UKOW040014220912

199457UK00001B/77/P